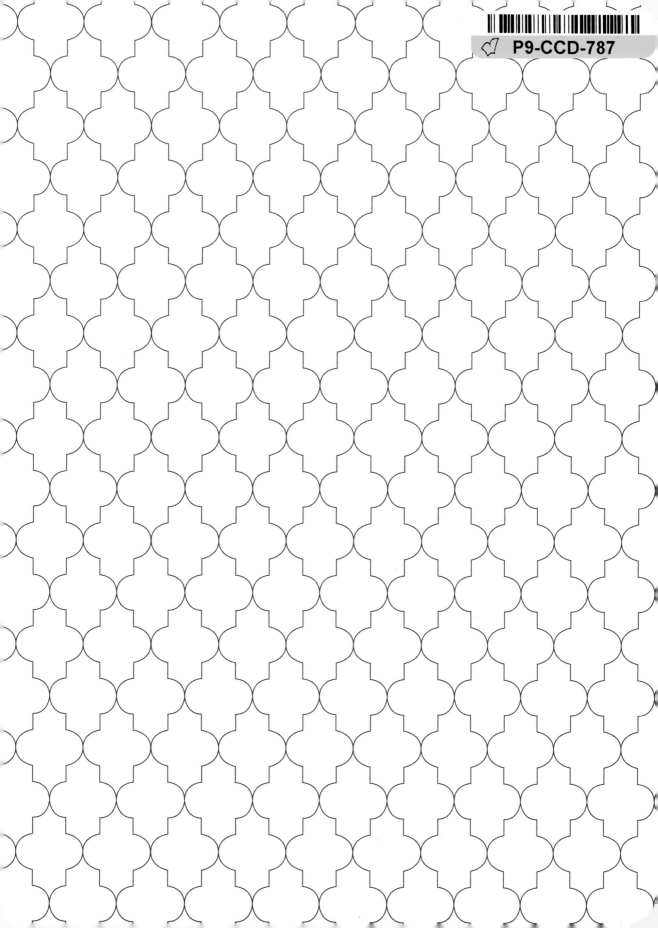

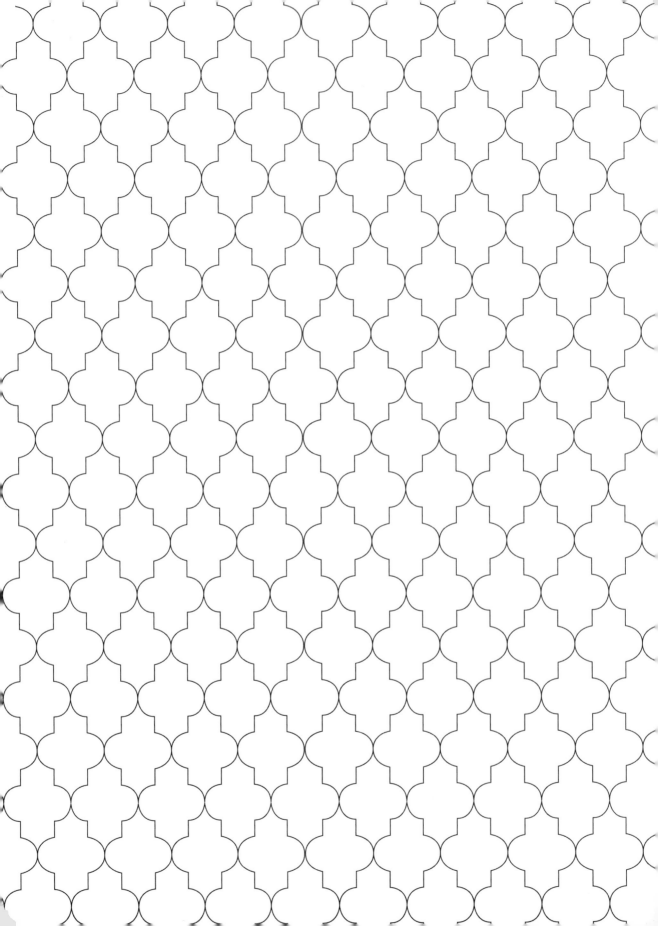

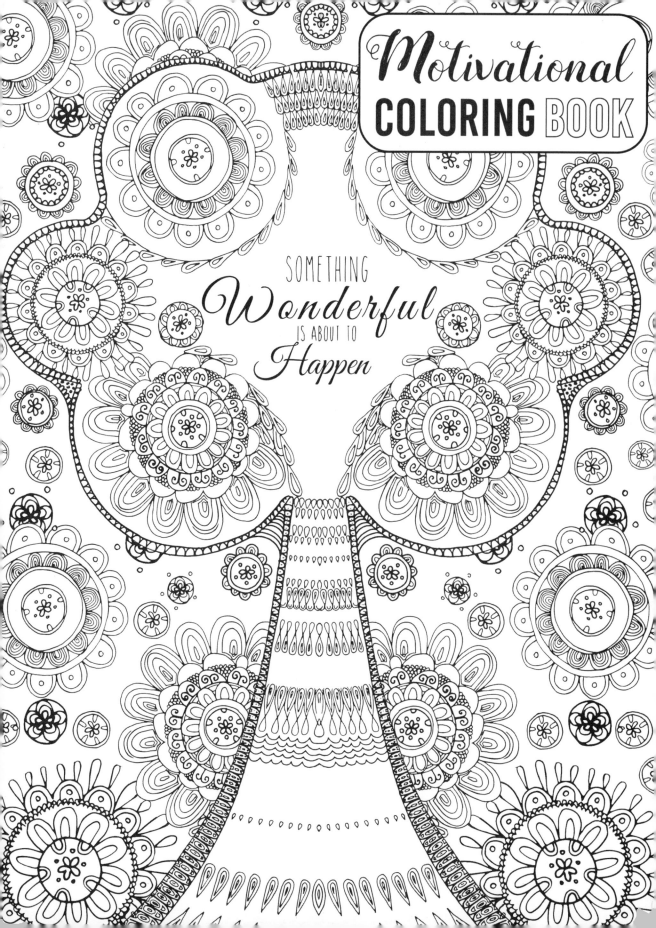

# Motivational
# COLORING BOOK

SOMETHING
*Wonderful*
IS ABOUT TO
*Happen*

© 2015 Piccadilly (USA) Inc.

This edition published by Piccadilly (USA) Inc.

Piccadilly (USA) Inc.
12702 Via Cortina, Suite 203
Del Mar, CA 92014
USA

10  9  8  7  6  5  4  3  2  1

Printed in China

ISBN-13: 978-1-60863-004-2

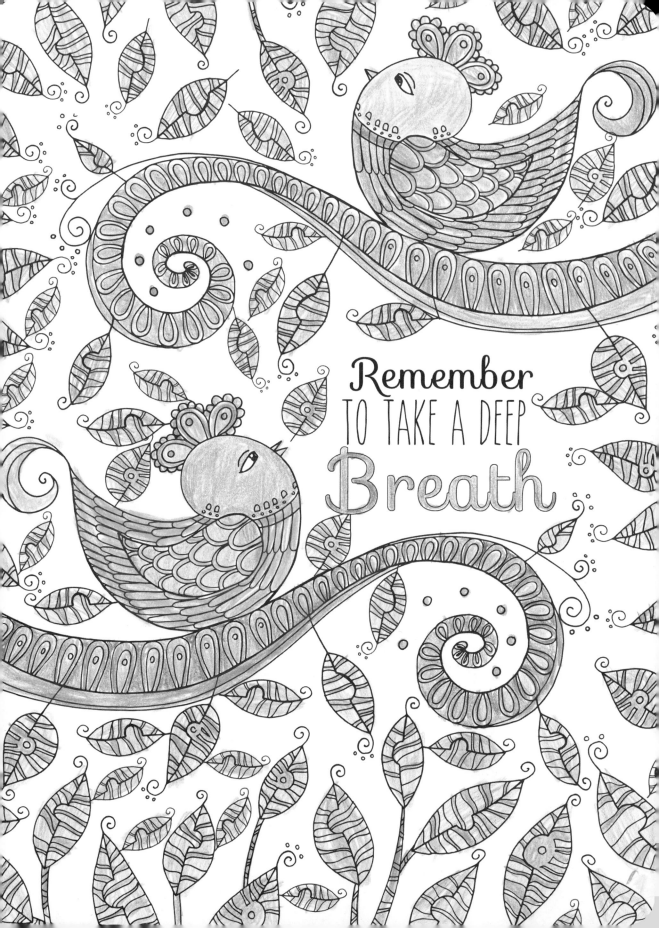

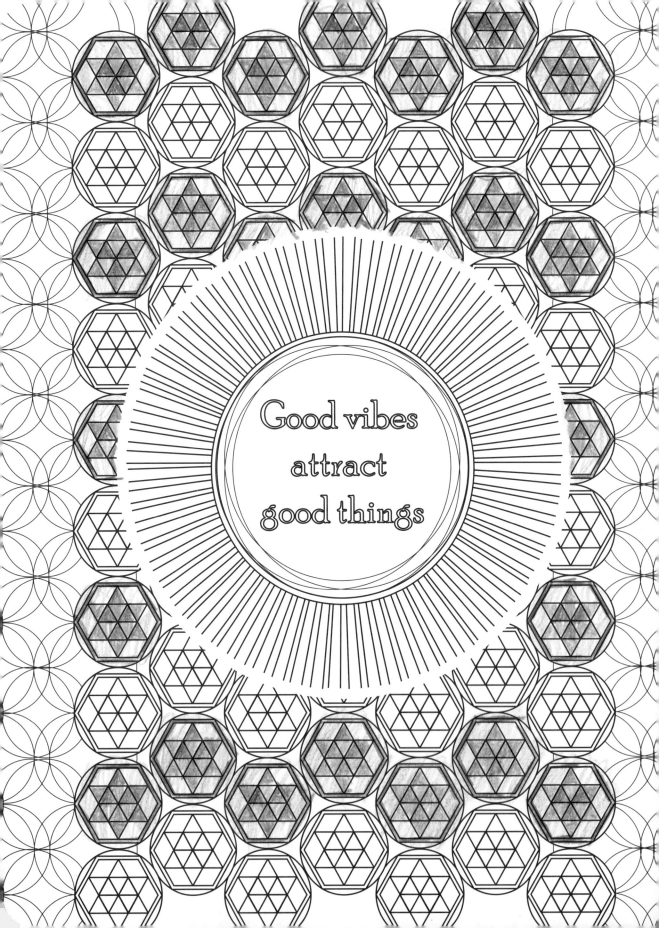

Good vibes
attract
good things

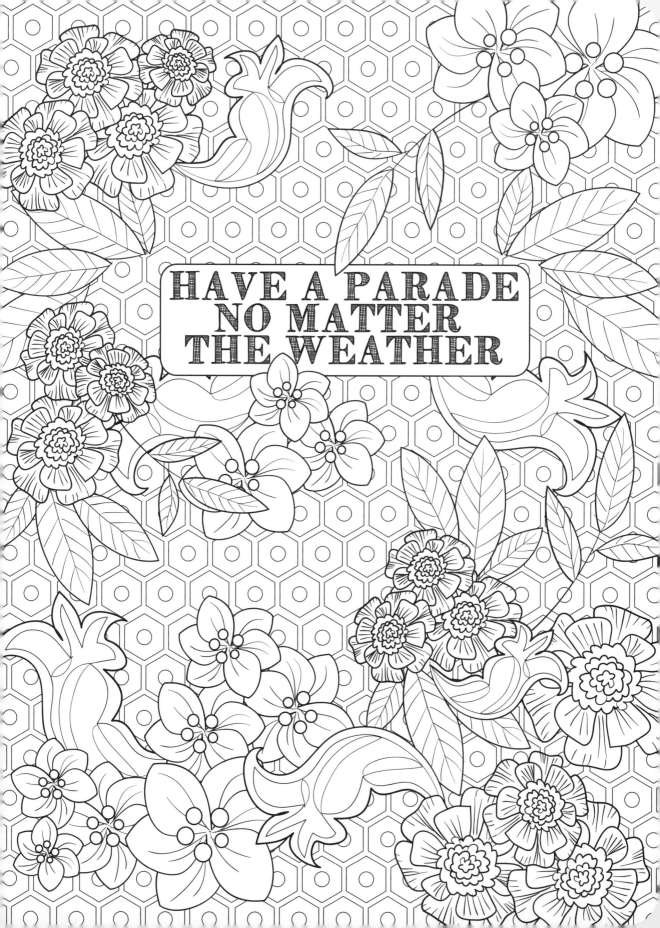

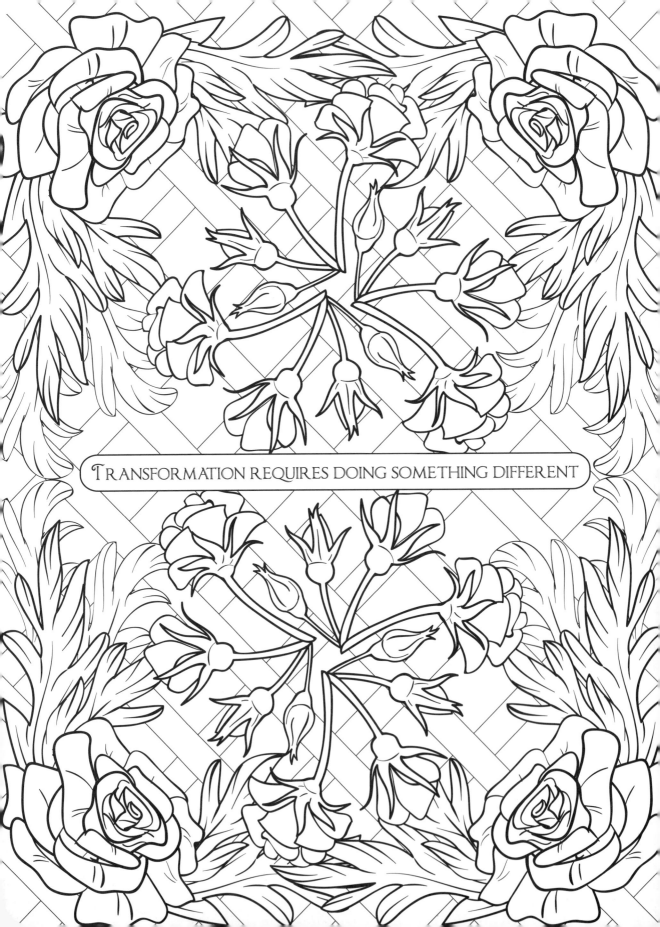

TRANSFORMATION REQUIRES DOING SOMETHING DIFFERENT

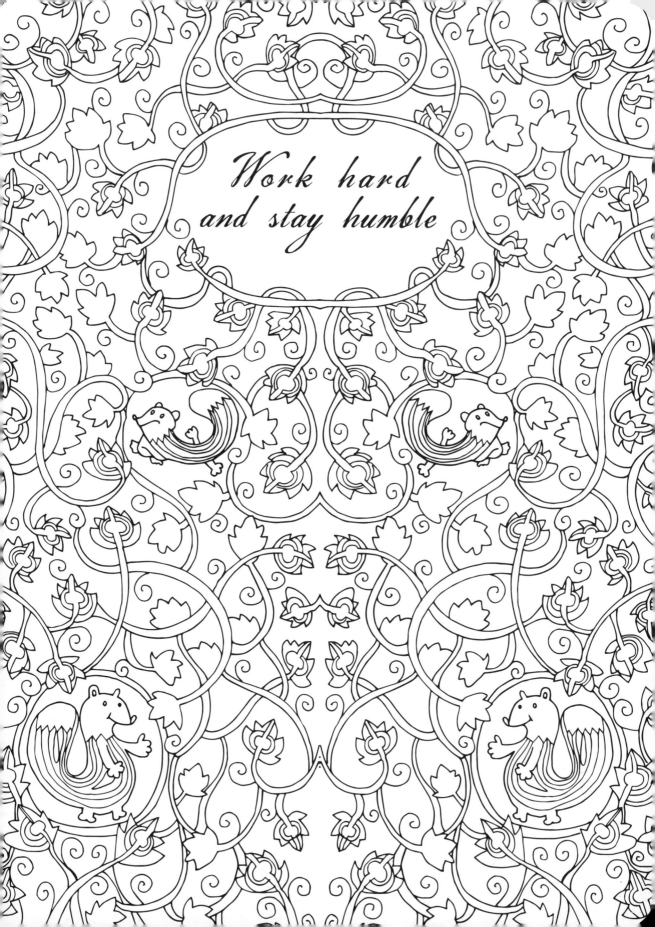

Work hard
and stay humble

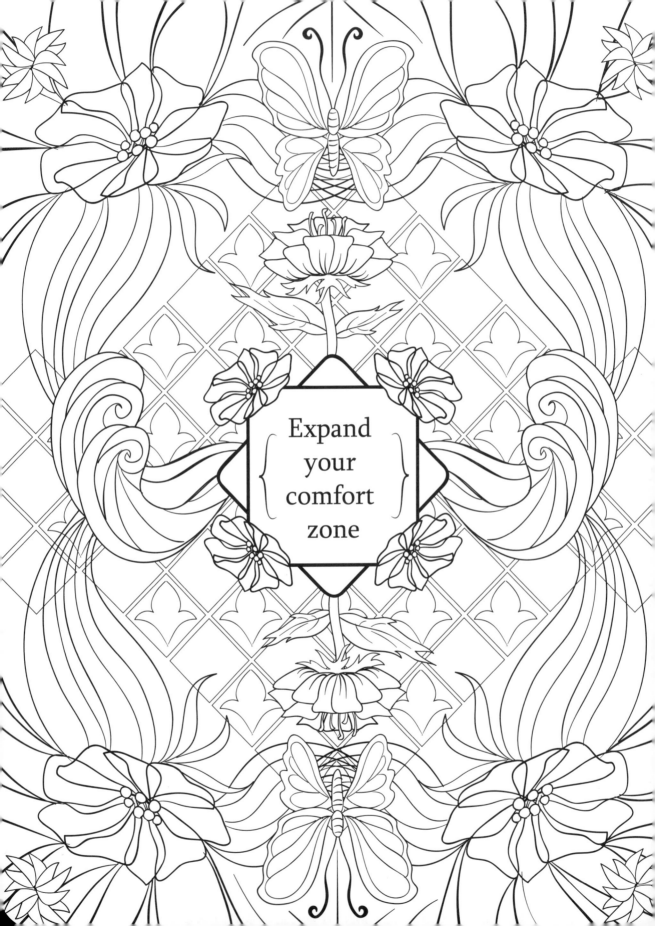

Expand
your
{ comfort }
zone

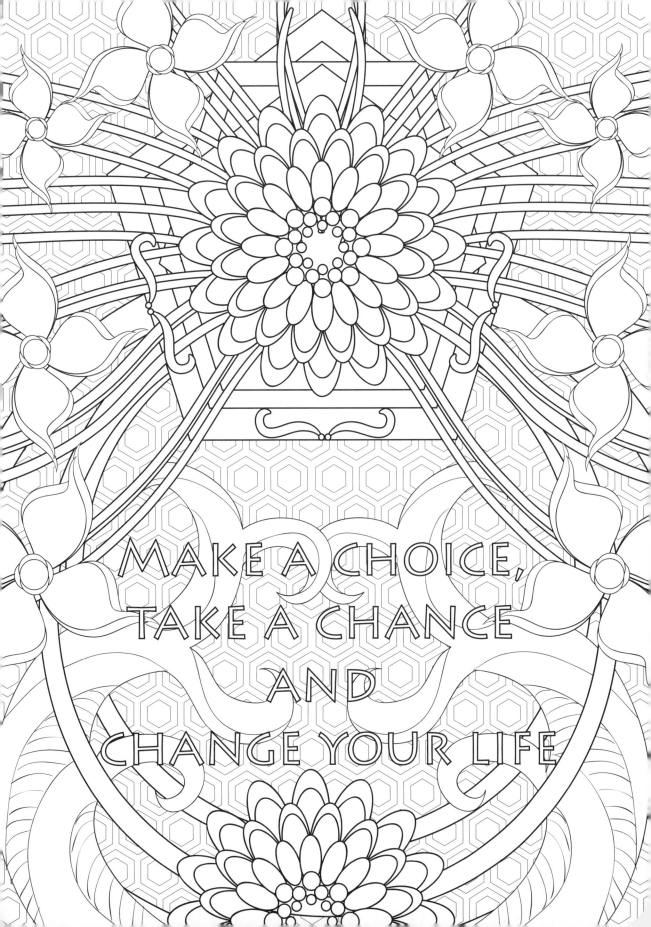

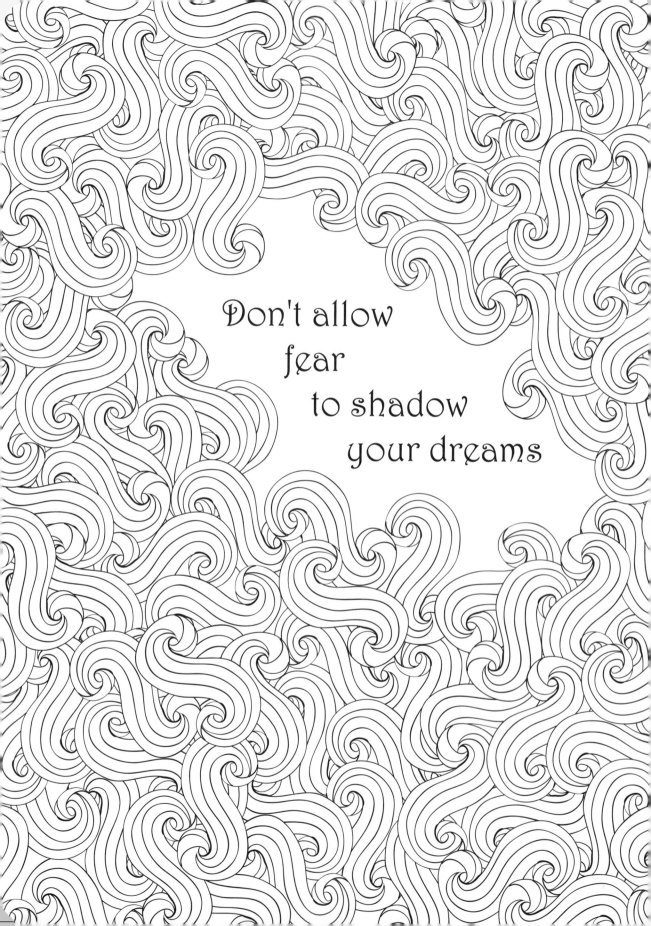

Don't allow
fear
to shadow
your dreams

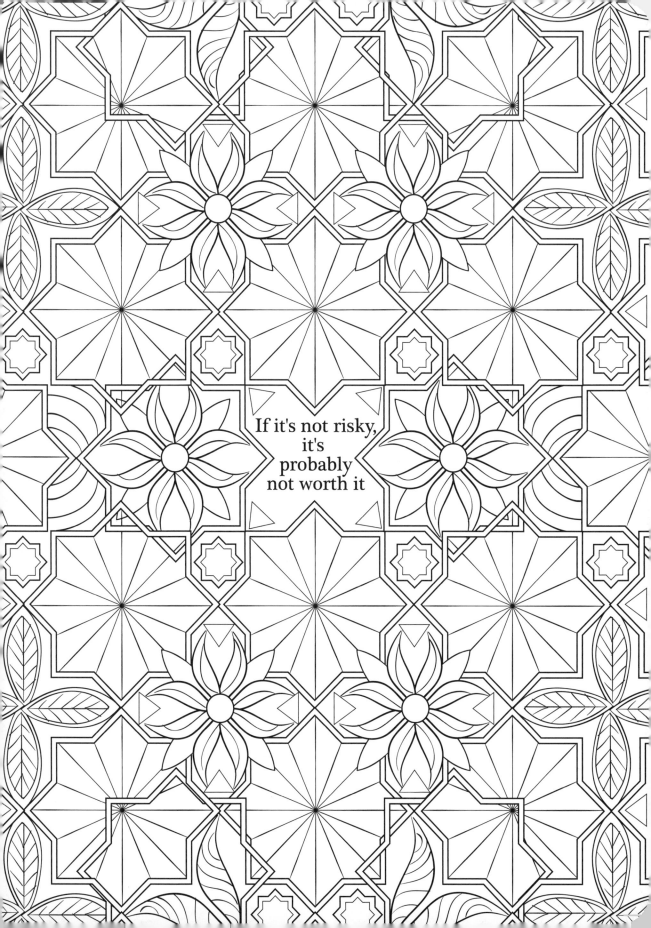

If it's not risky,
it's
probably
not worth it

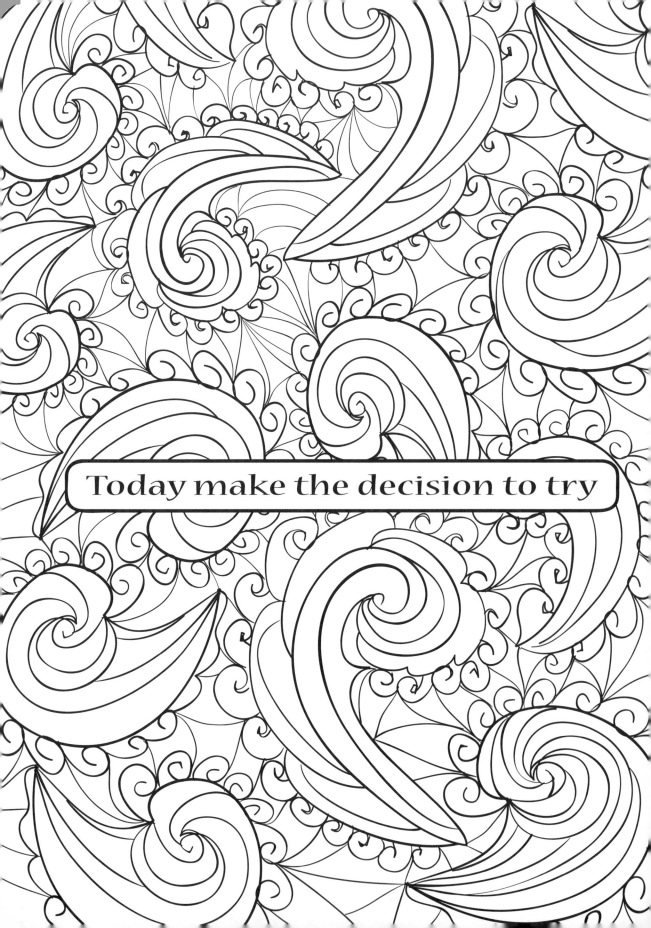

Today make the decision to try

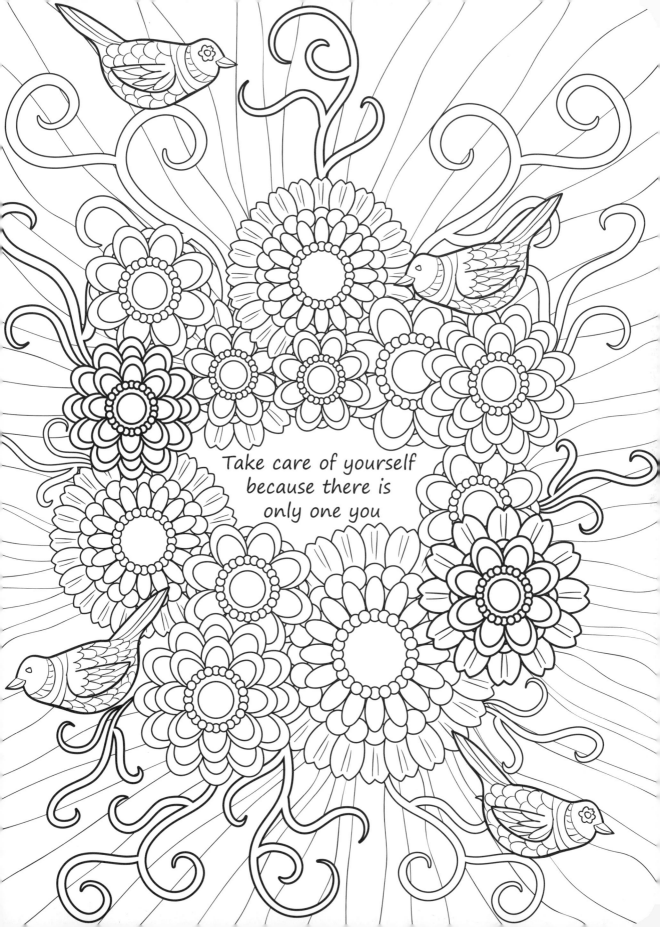

Take care of yourself
because there is
only one you

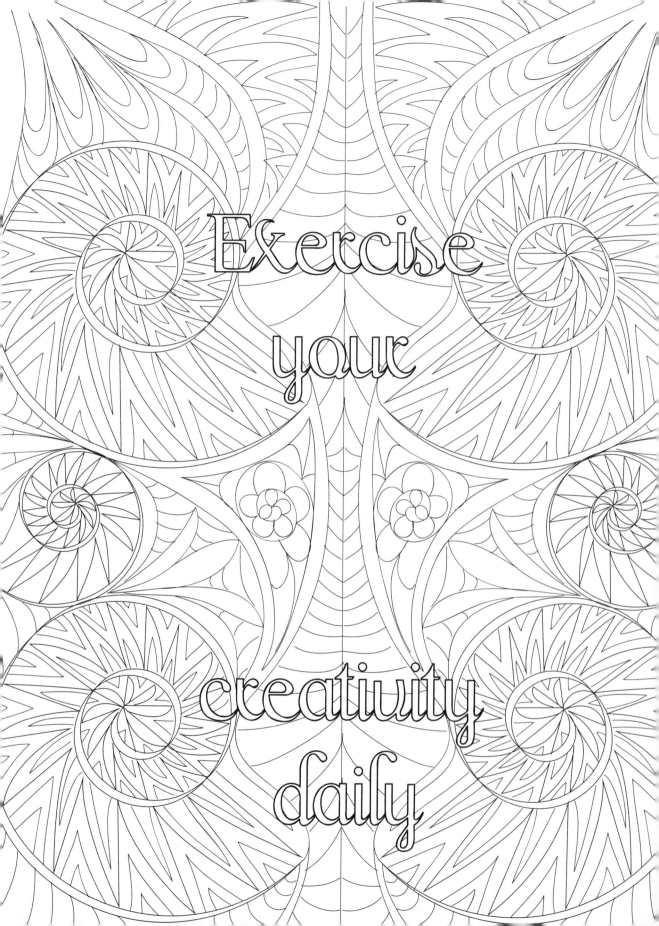

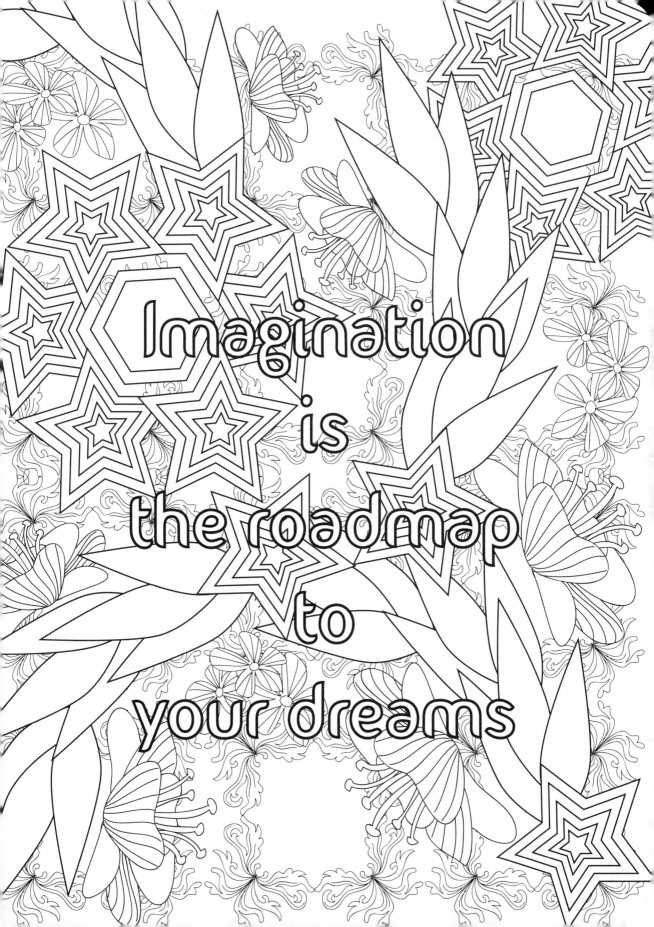

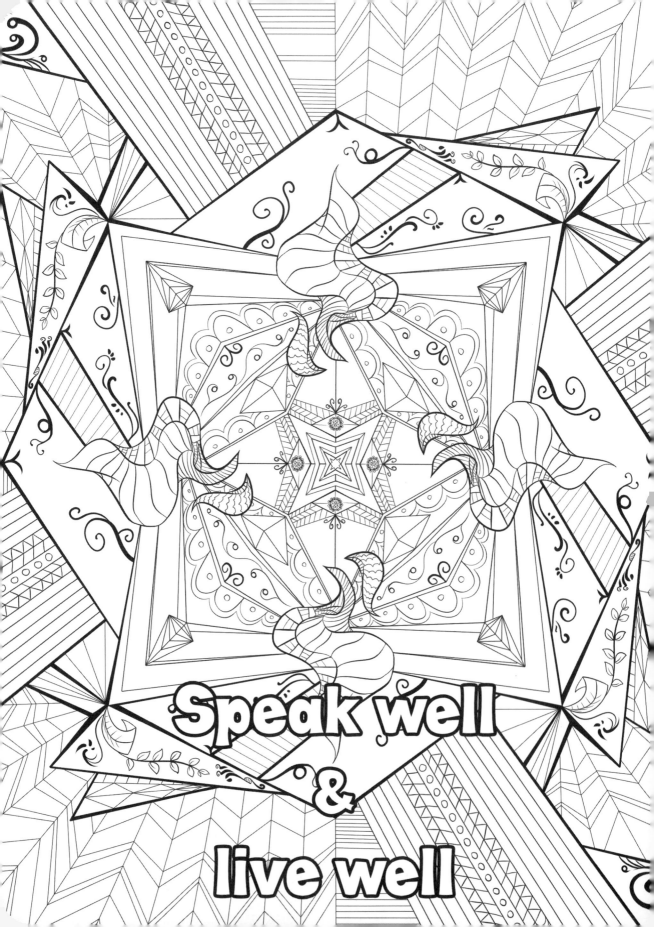

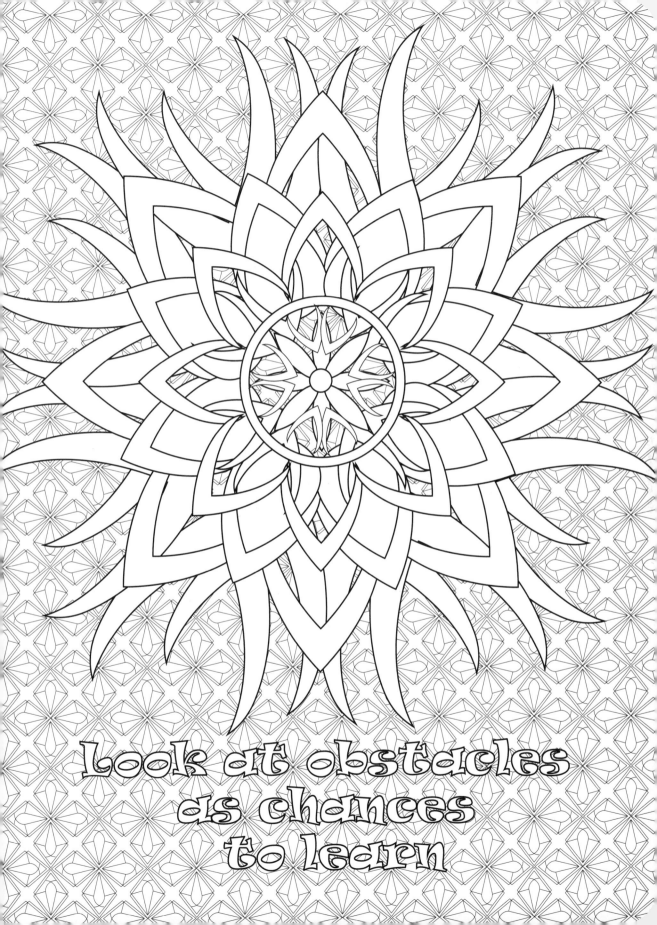

Look at obstacles
as chances
to learn

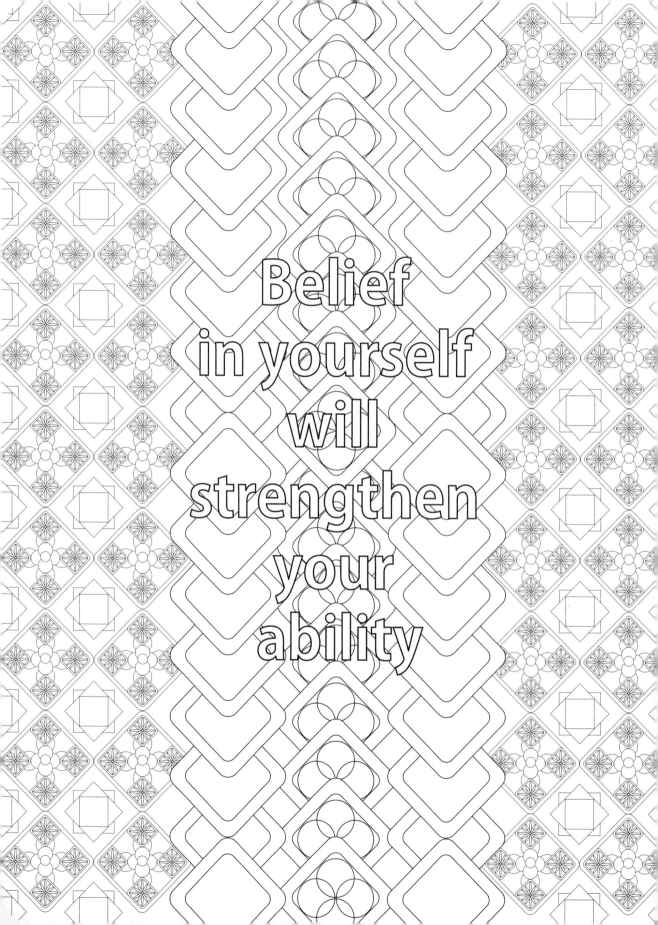

Belief in yourself will strengthen your ability

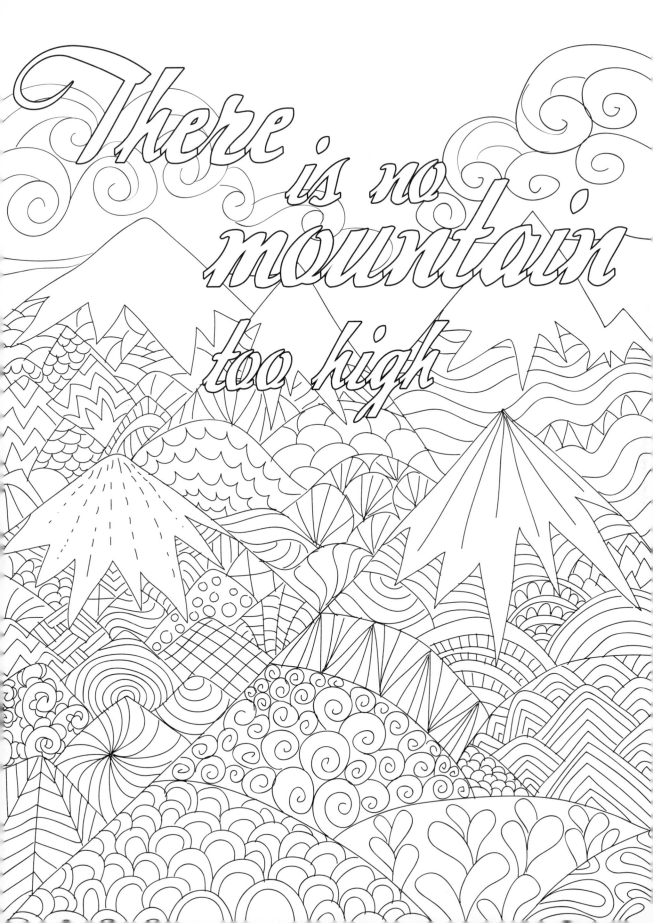

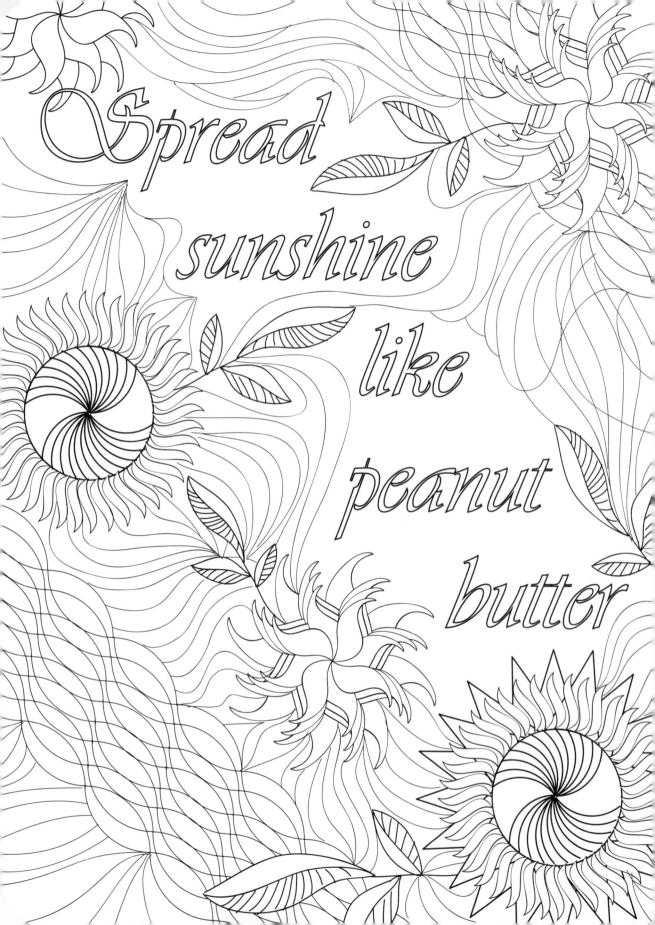

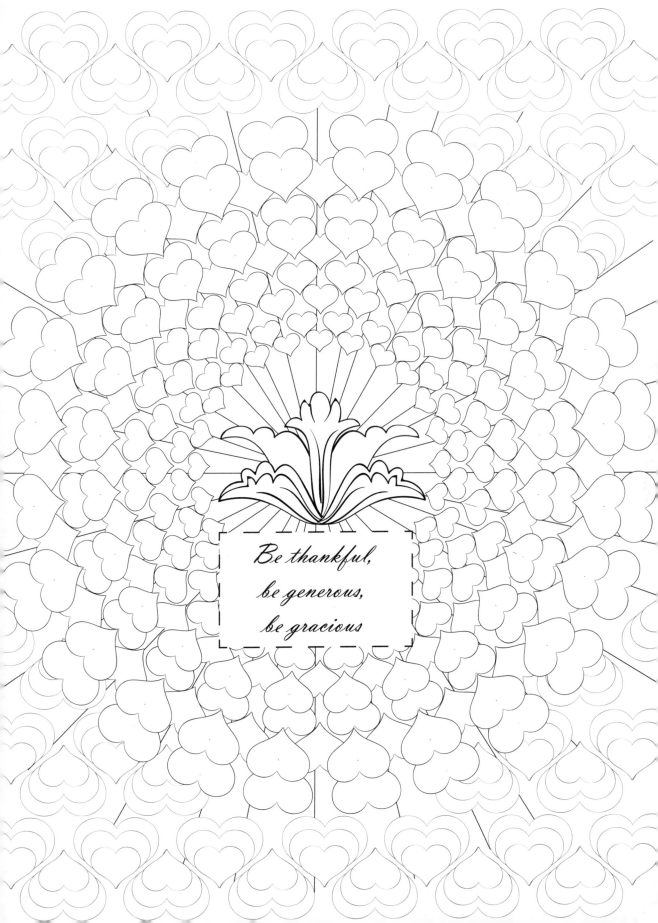

Be thankful,
be generous,
be gracious

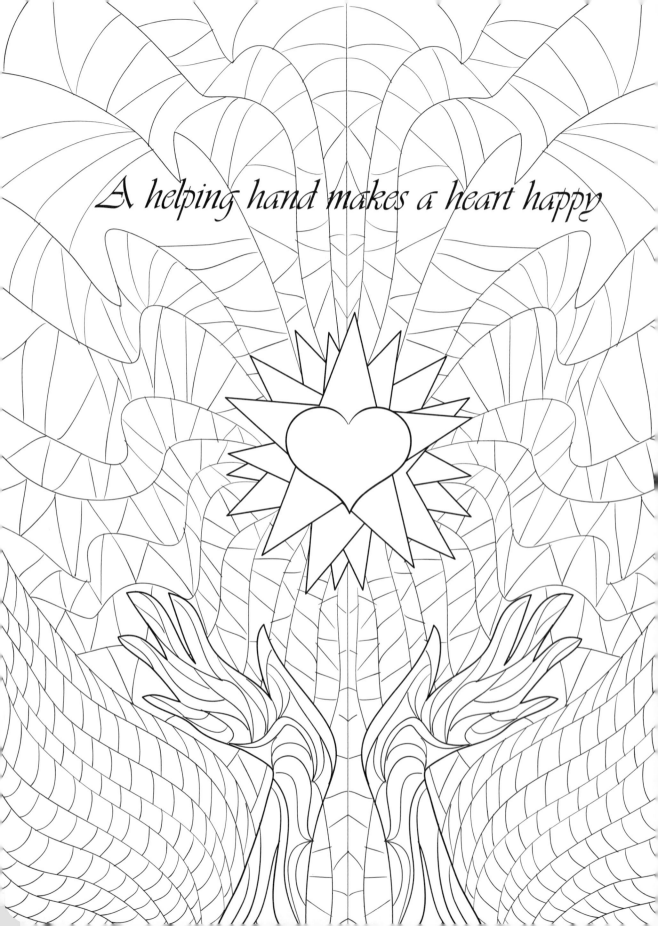

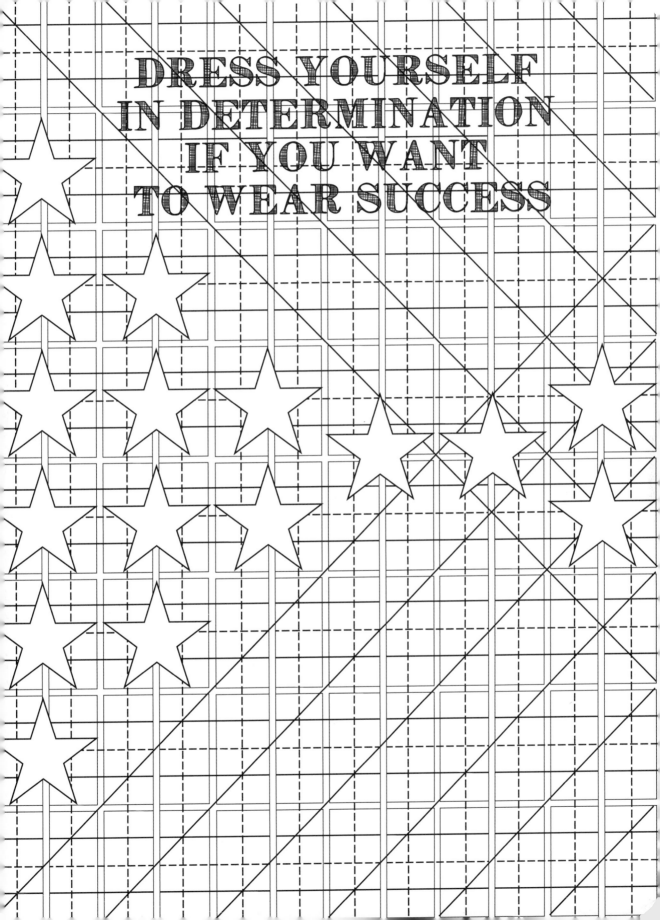

DRESS YOURSELF
IN DETERMINATION
IF YOU WANT
TO WEAR SUCCESS

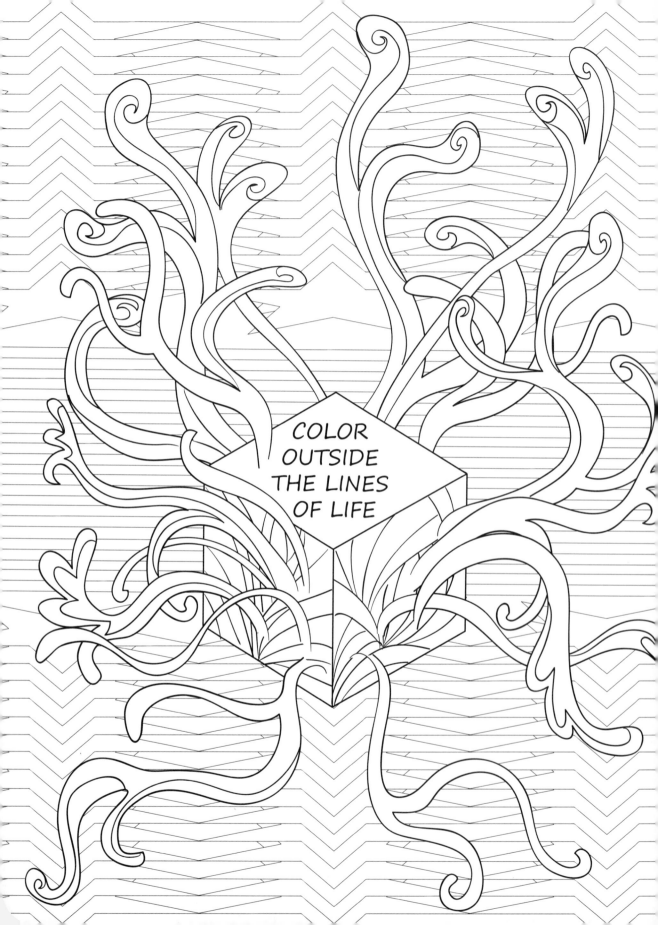

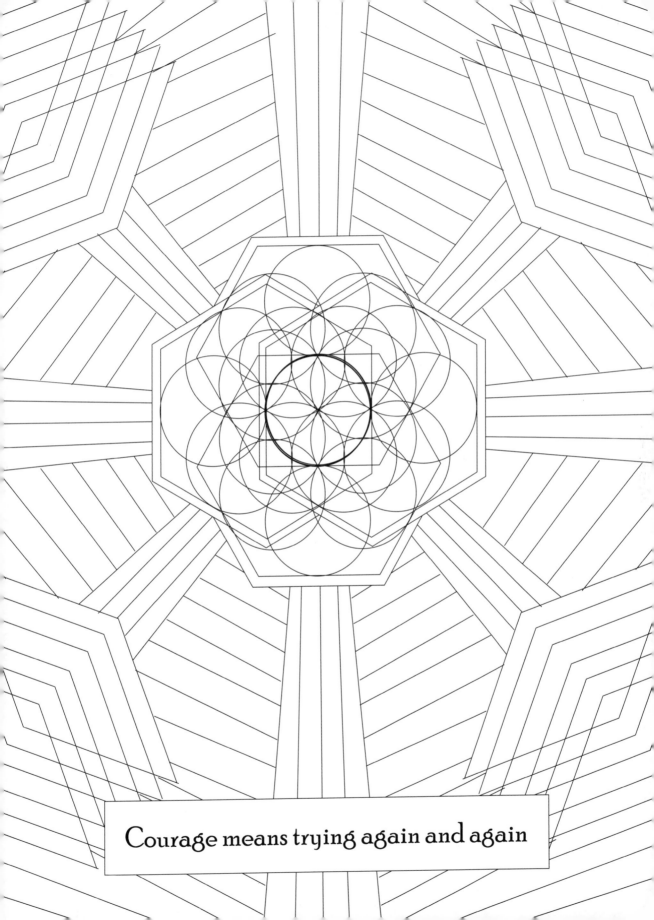

Courage means trying again and again

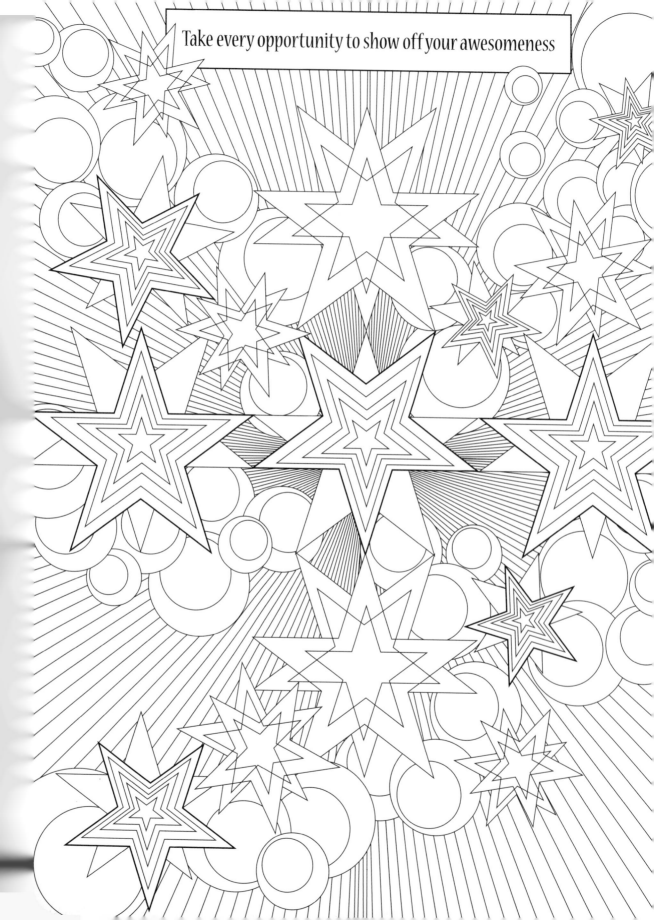

Take every opportunity to show off your awesomeness

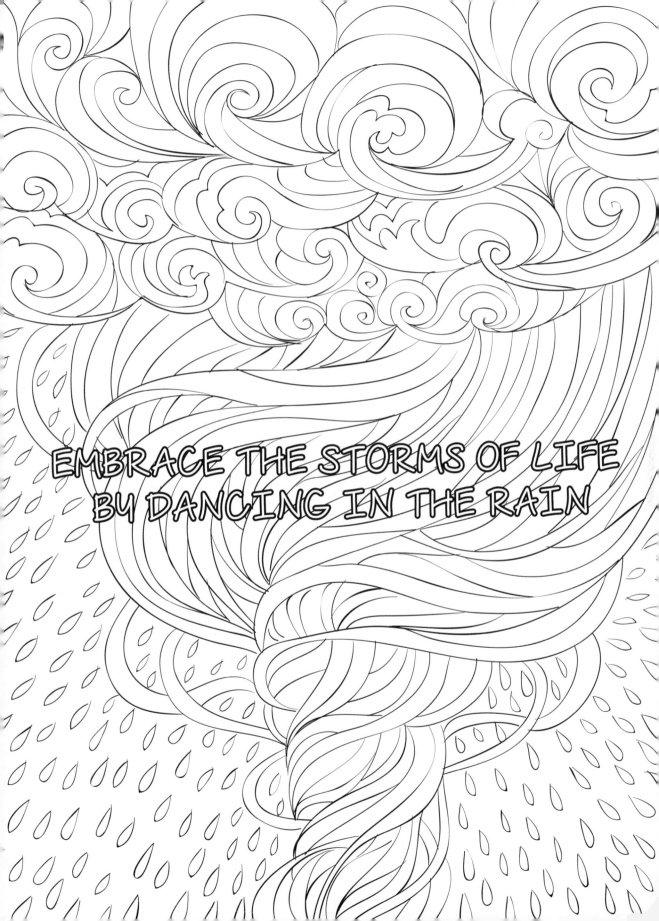

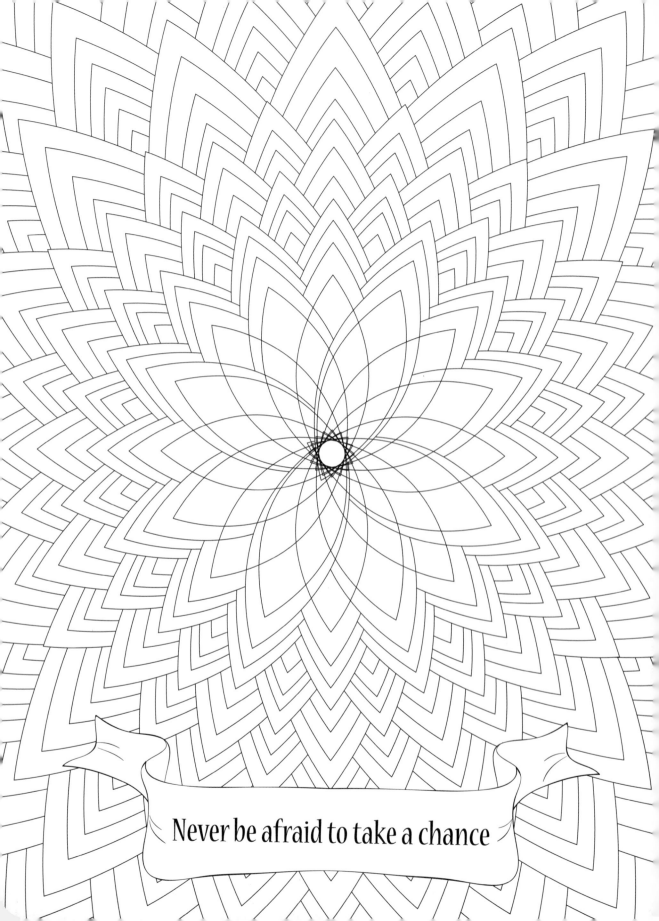

Never be afraid to take a chance

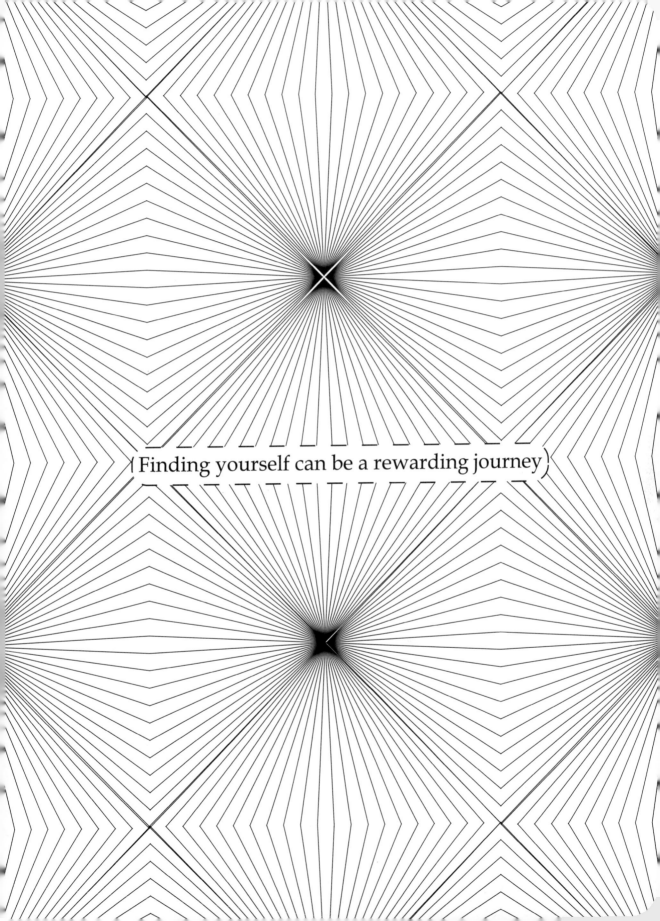

Finding yourself can be a rewarding journey

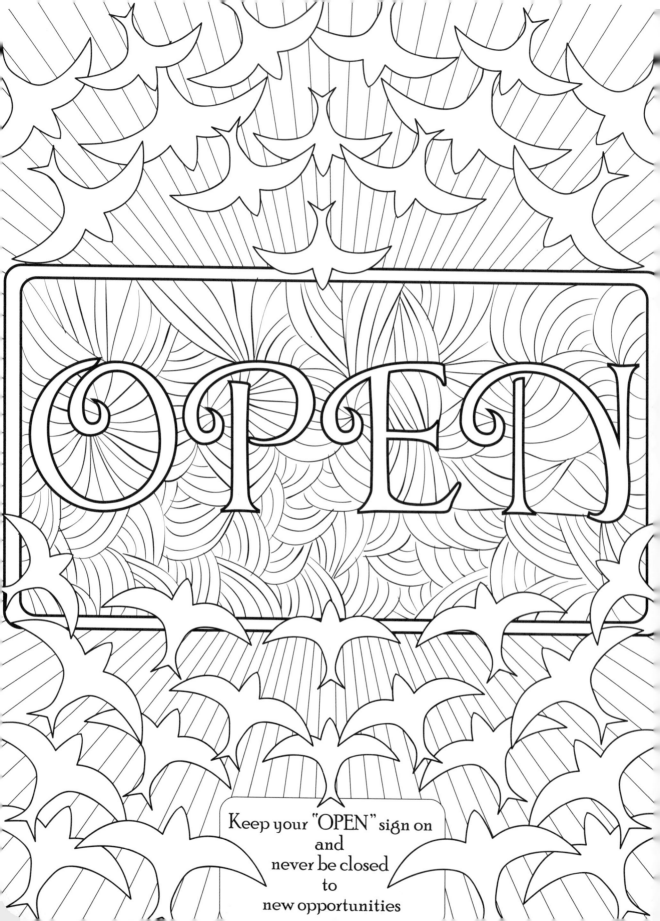

OPEN

Keep your "OPEN" sign on
and
never be closed
to
new opportunities

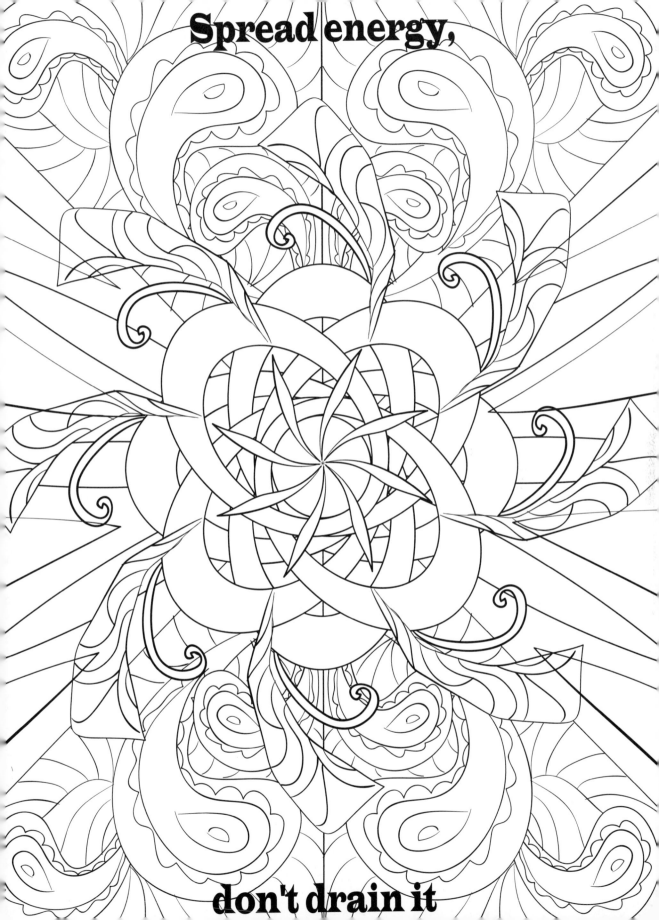

Spread energy,

don't drain it

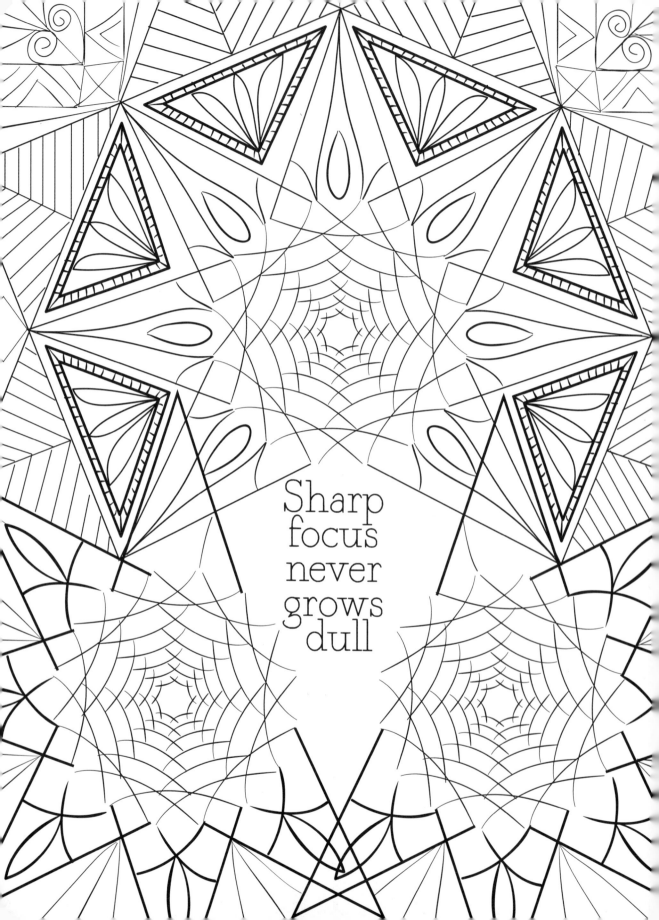

Sharp
focus
never
grows
dull

Follow your bliss

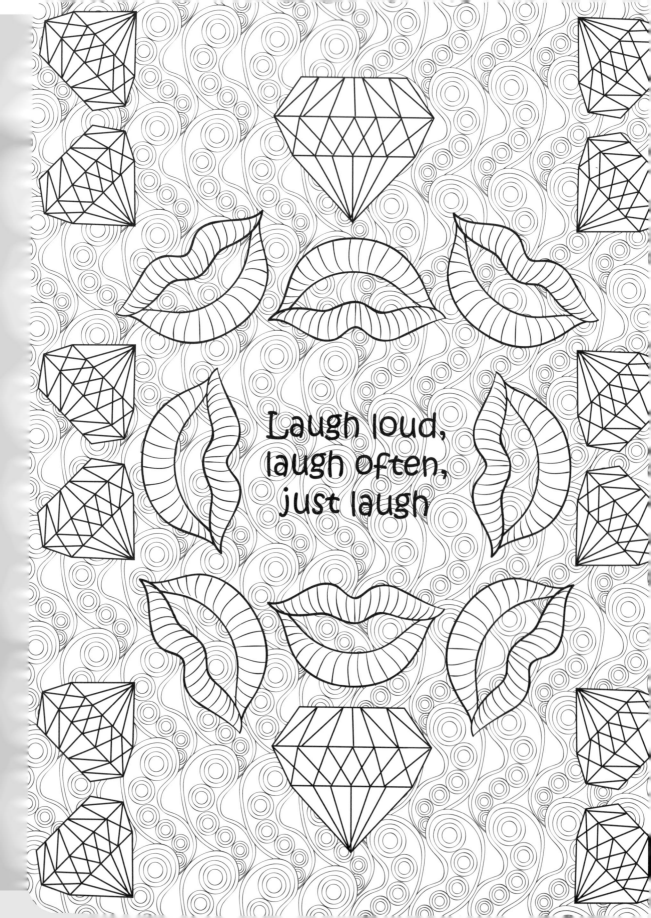

Laugh loud,
laugh often,
just laugh

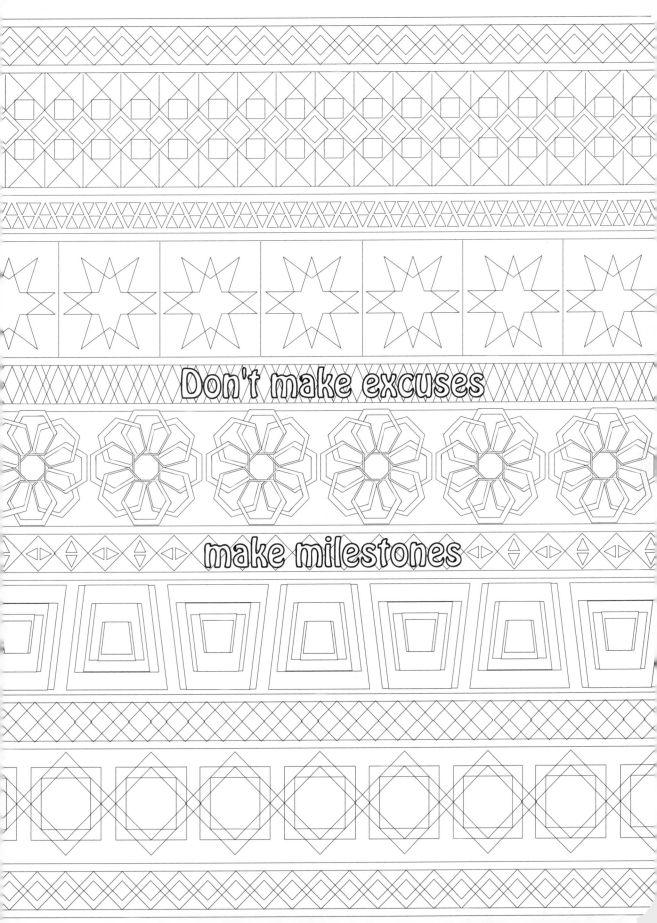

Don't make excuses

make milestones

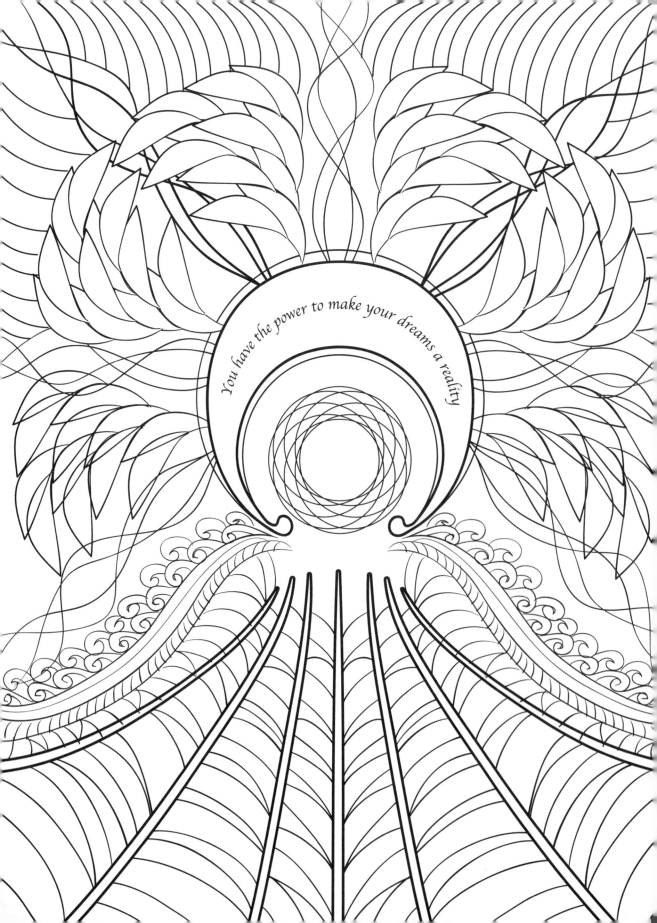

You have the power to make your dreams a reality

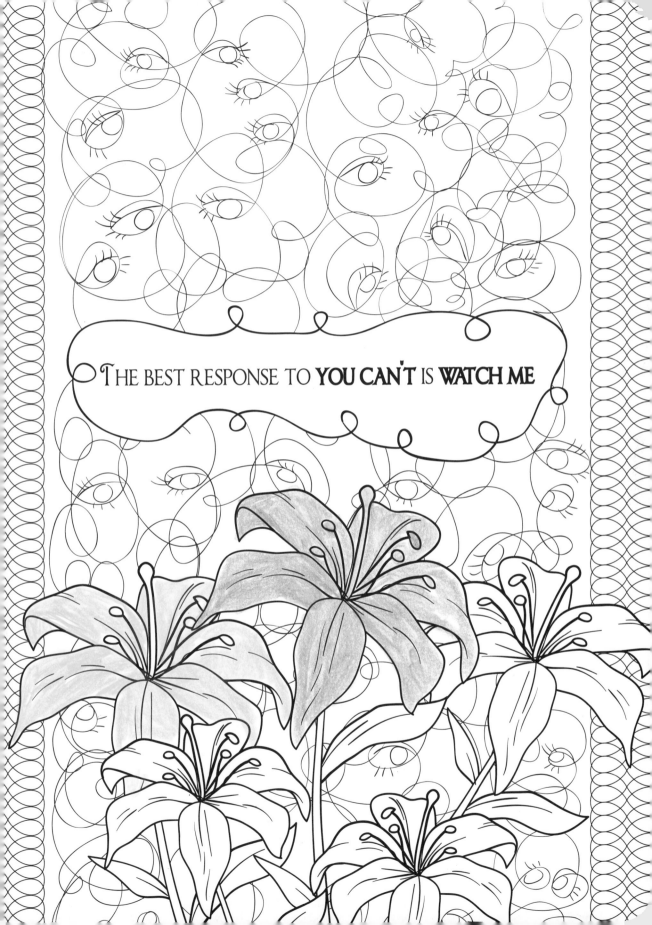

THE BEST RESPONSE TO **YOU CAN'T** IS **WATCH ME**

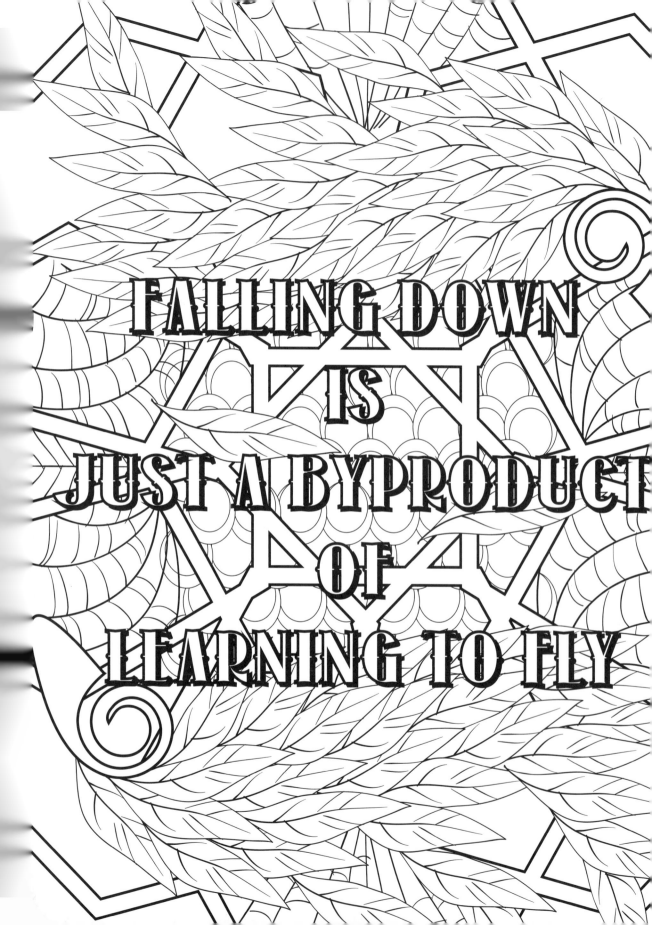

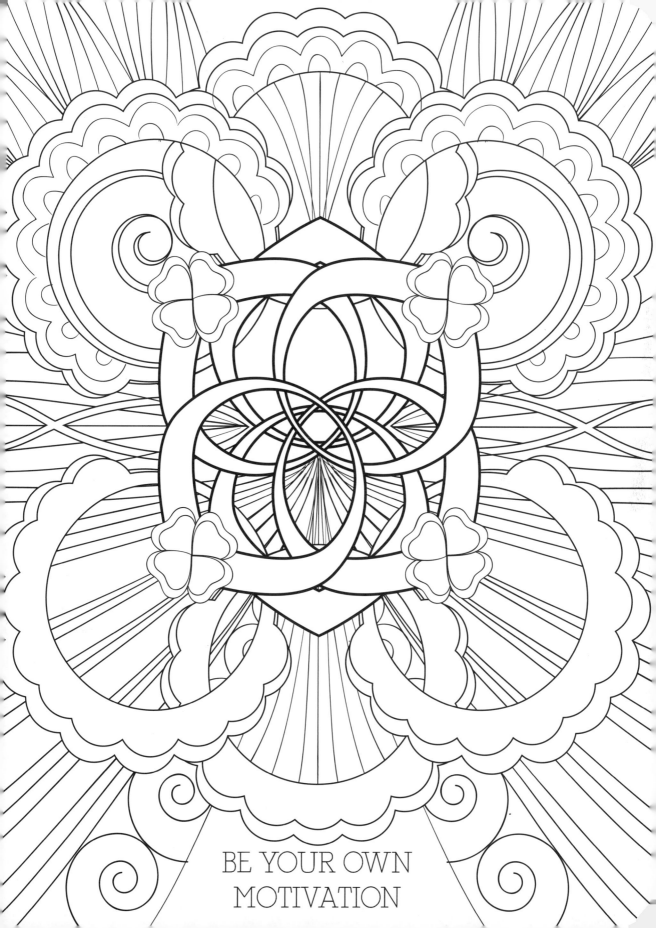

BE YOUR OWN
MOTIVATION

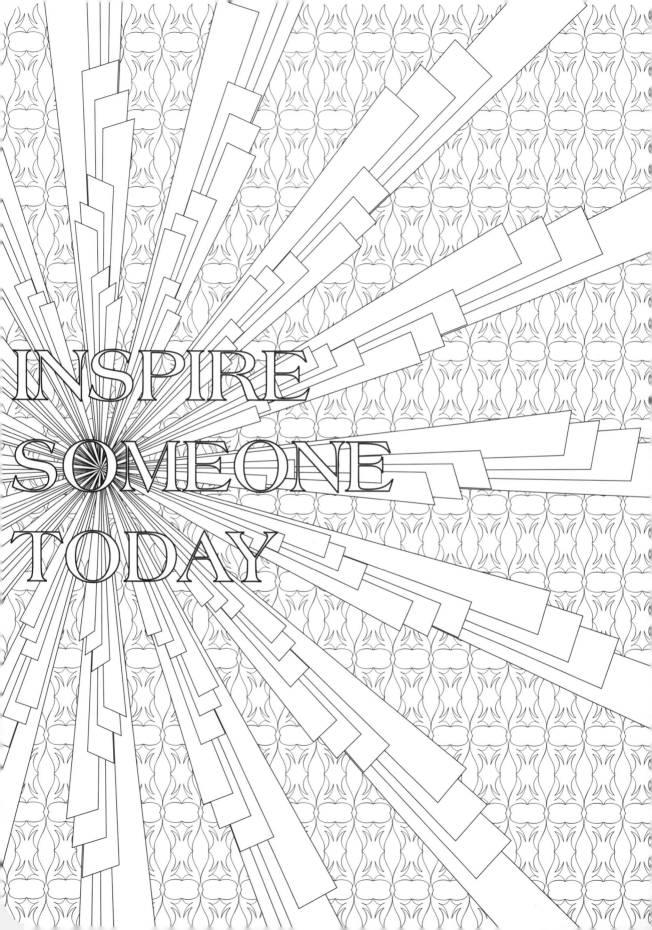

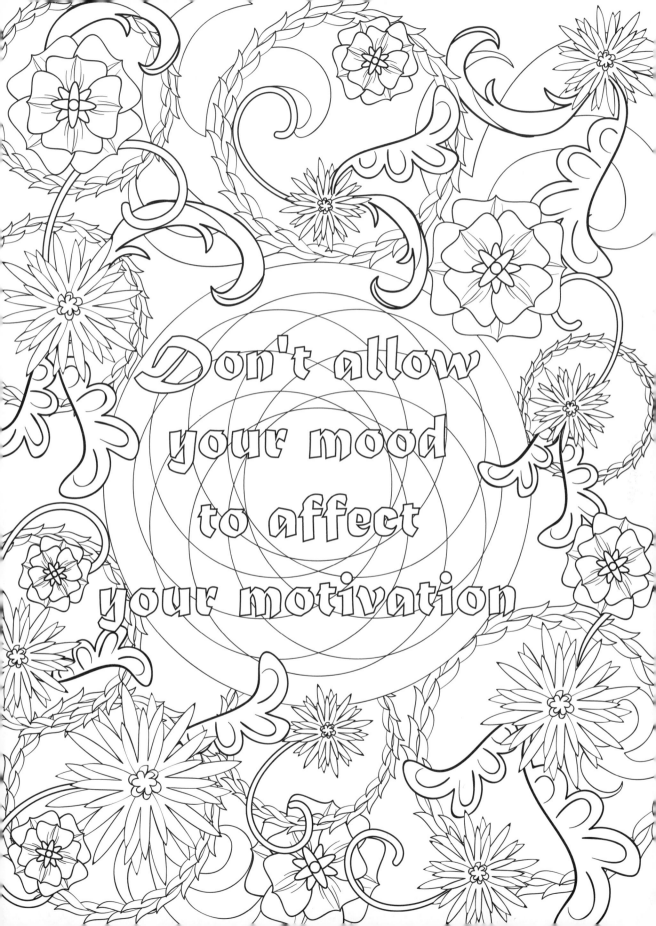

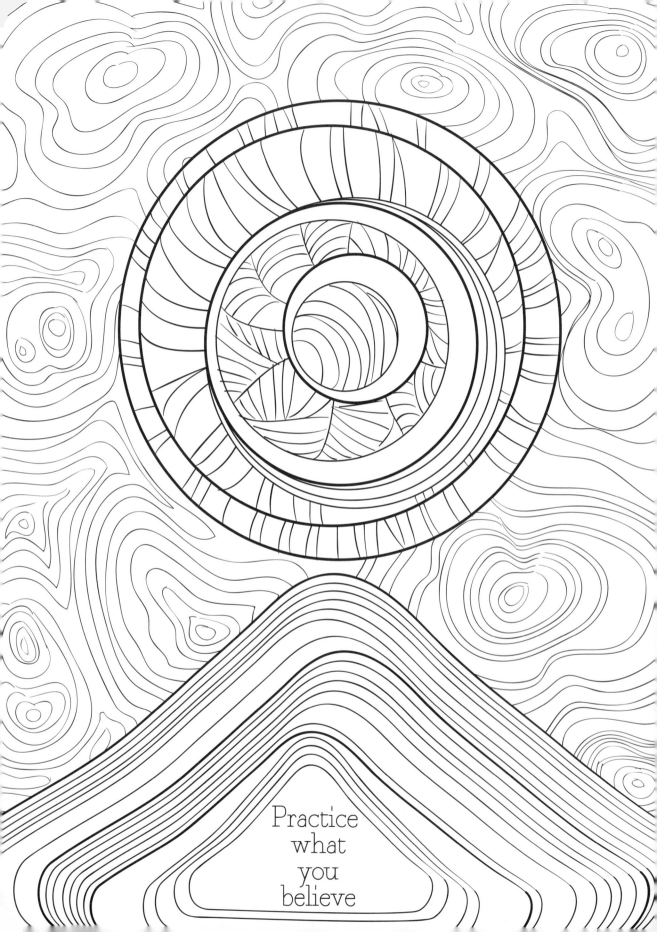

Practice
what
you
believe

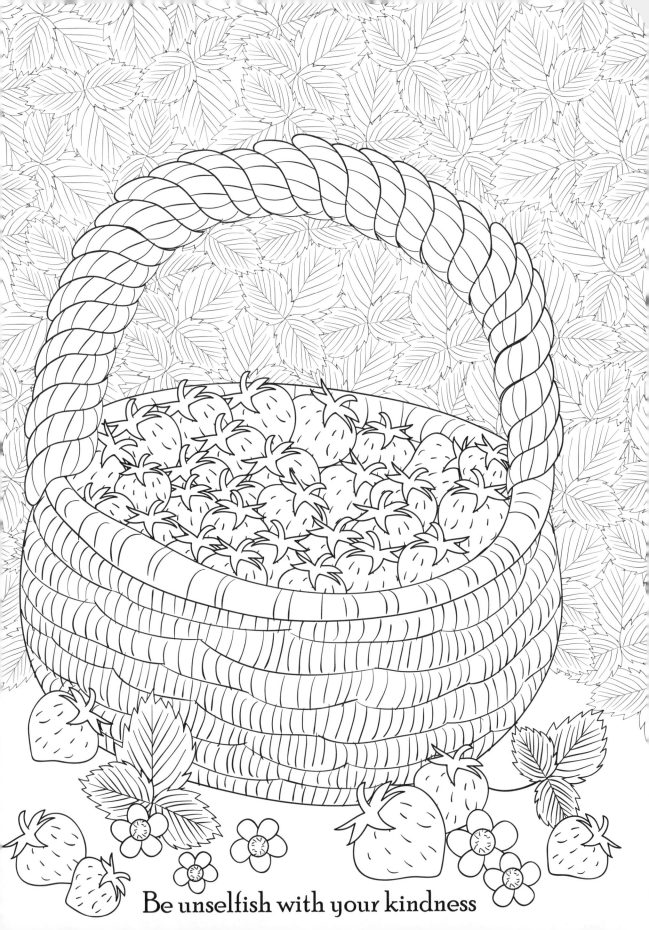

Be unselfish with your kindness

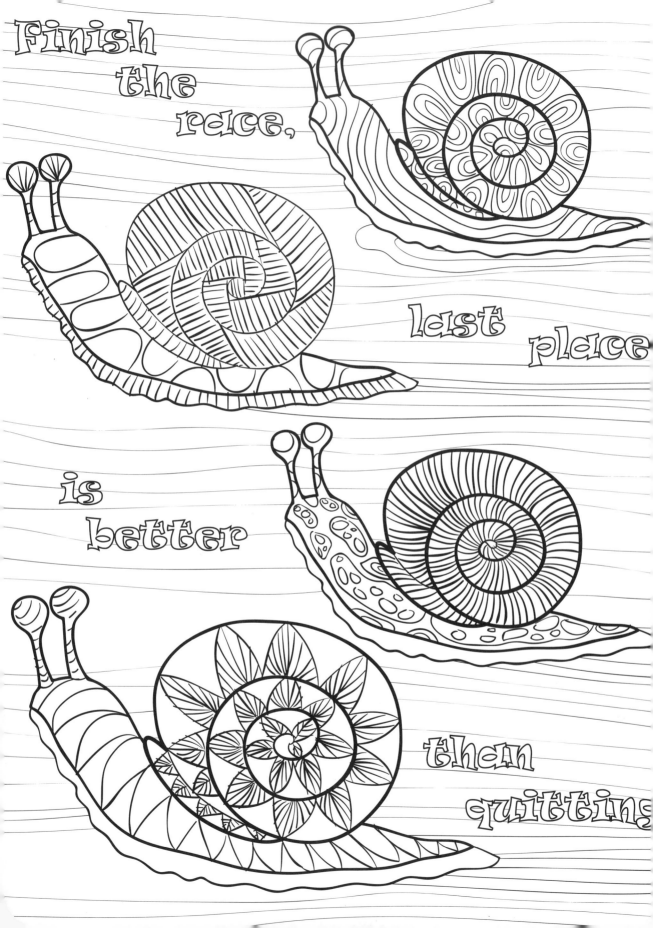

Finish the race, last place is better than quitting

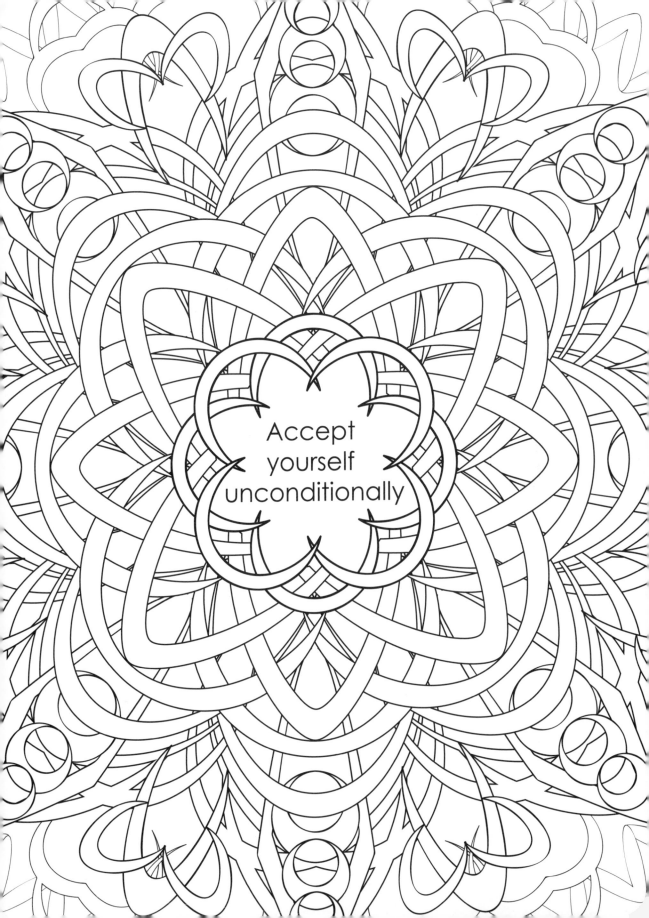

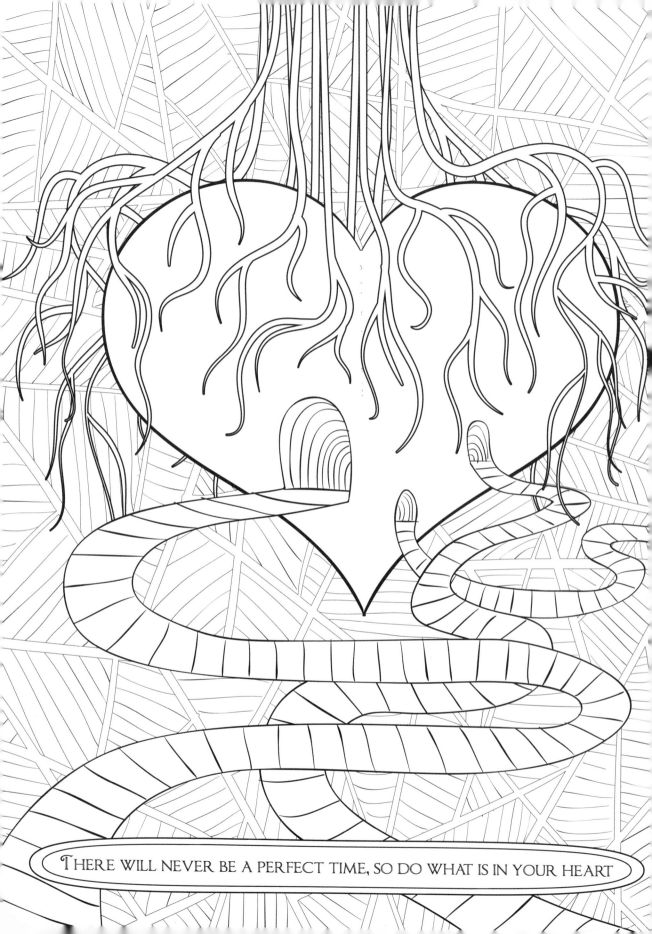

THERE WILL NEVER BE A PERFECT TIME, SO DO WHAT IS IN YOUR HEART

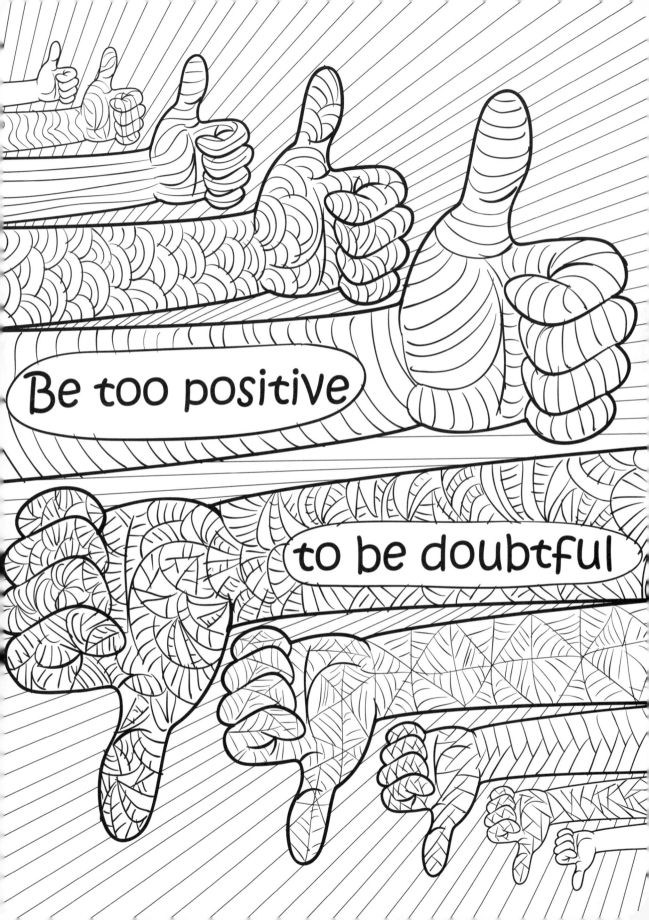

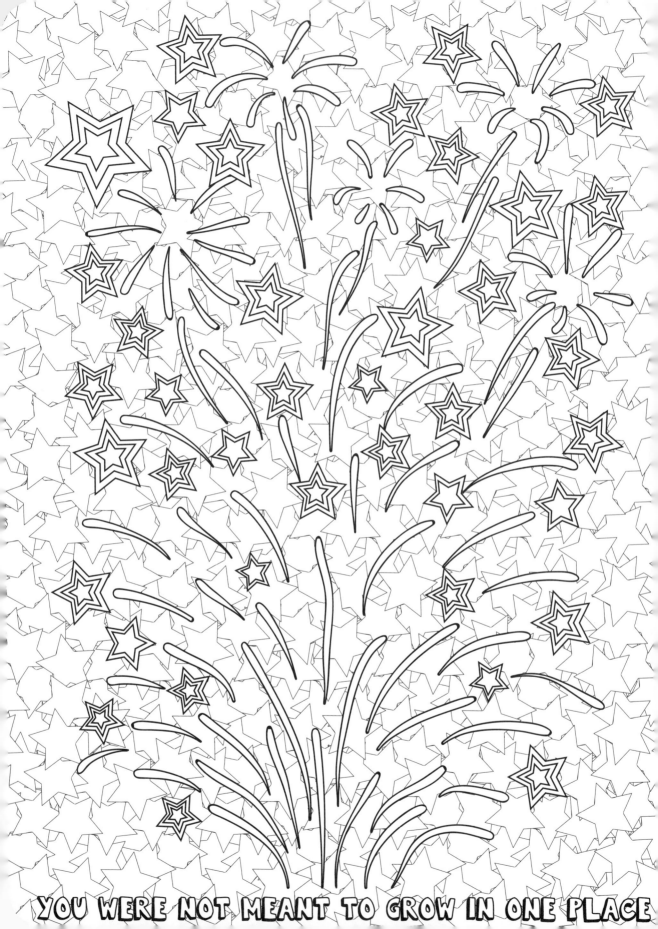

YOU WERE NOT MEANT TO GROW IN ONE PLACE

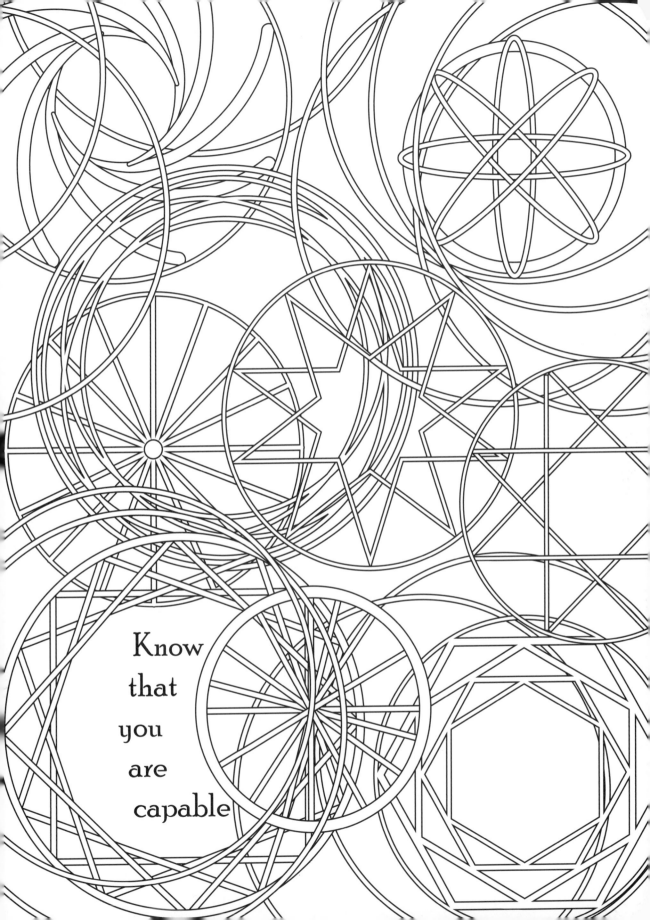

Know
that
you
are
capable

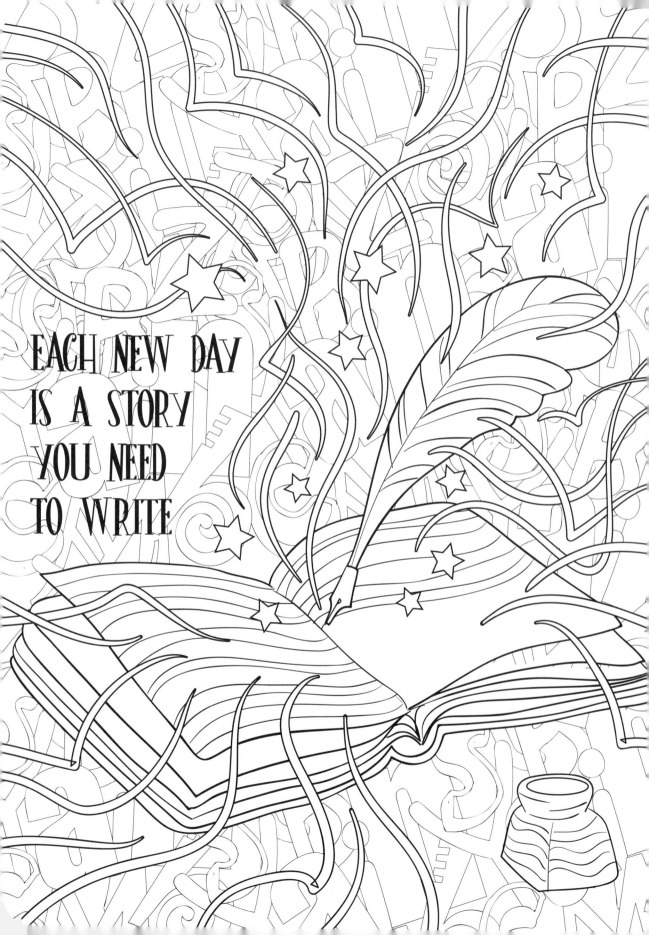

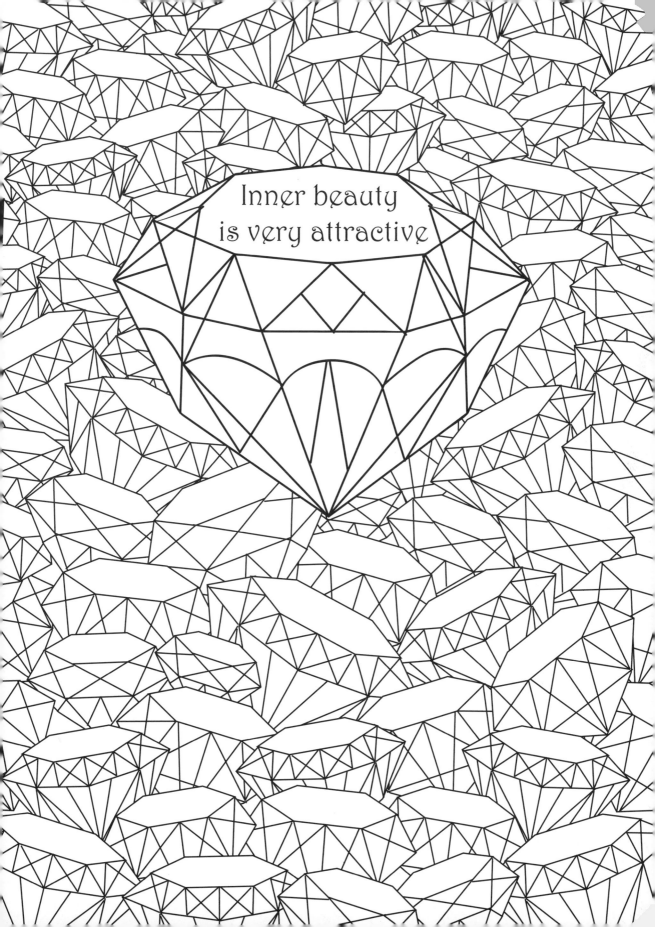

Inner beauty
is very attractive

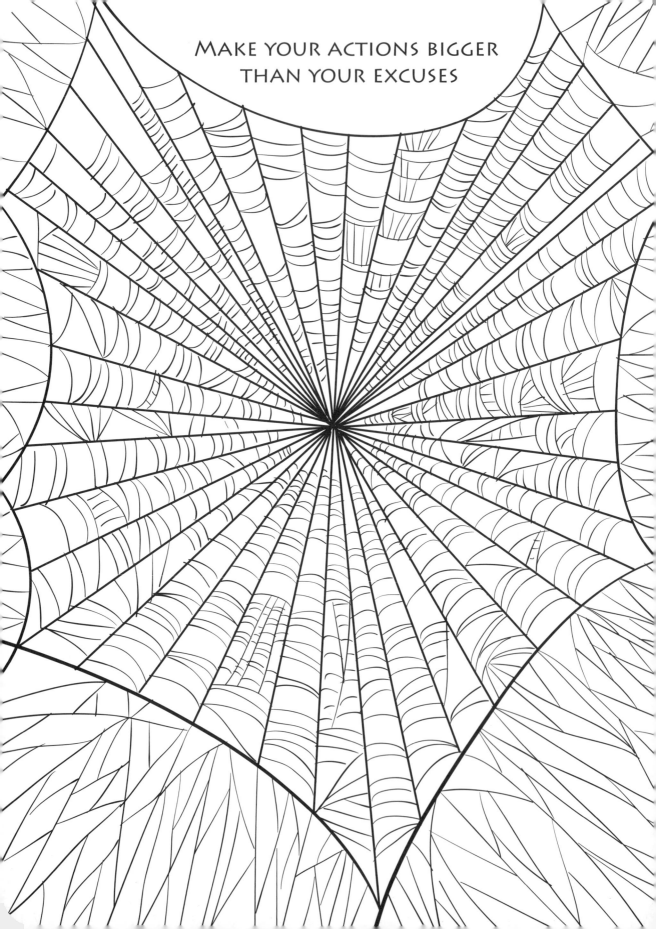

MAKE YOUR ACTIONS BIGGER
THAN YOUR EXCUSES

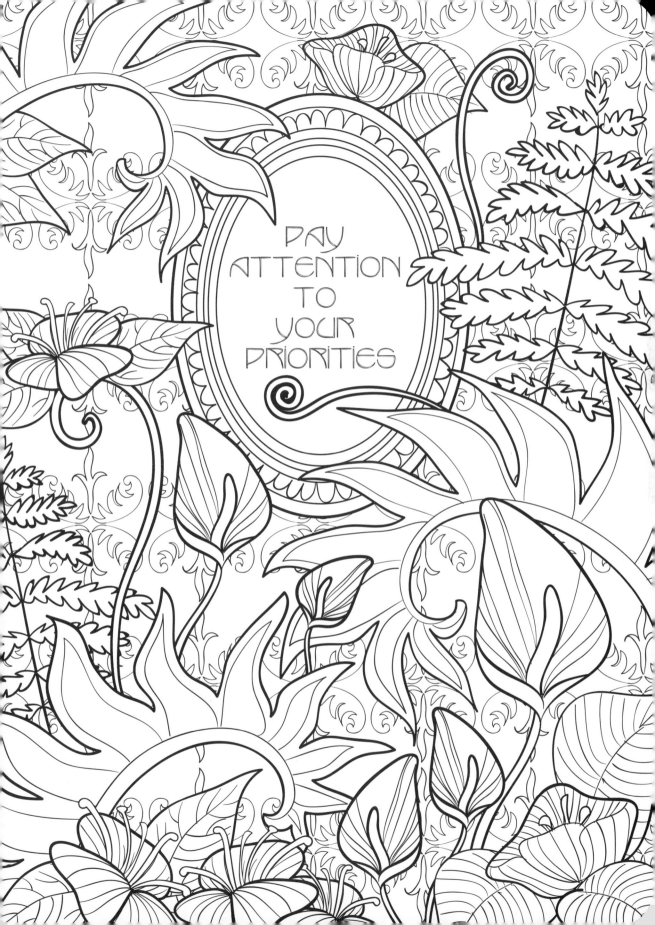

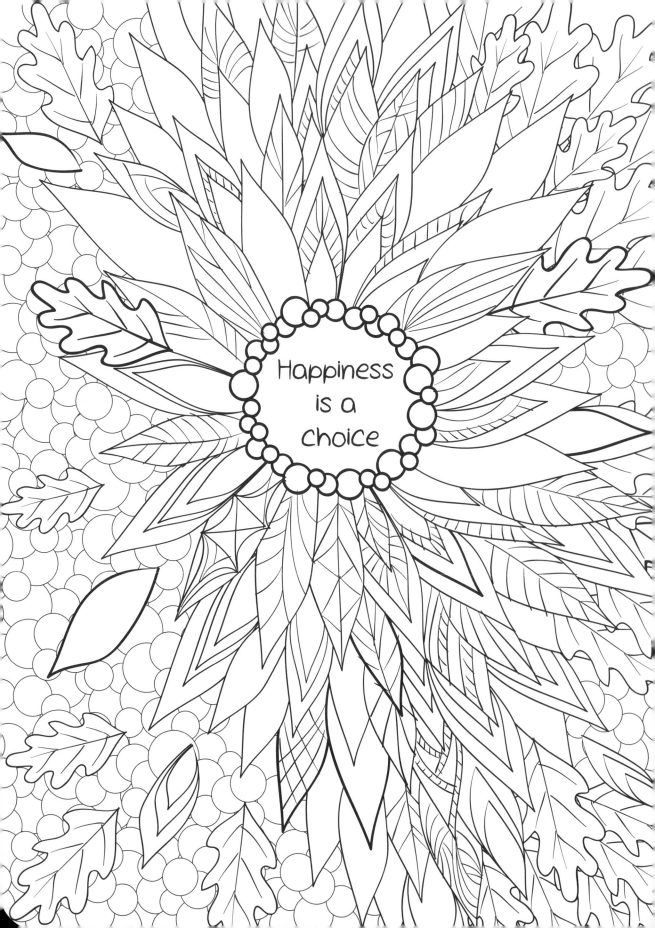

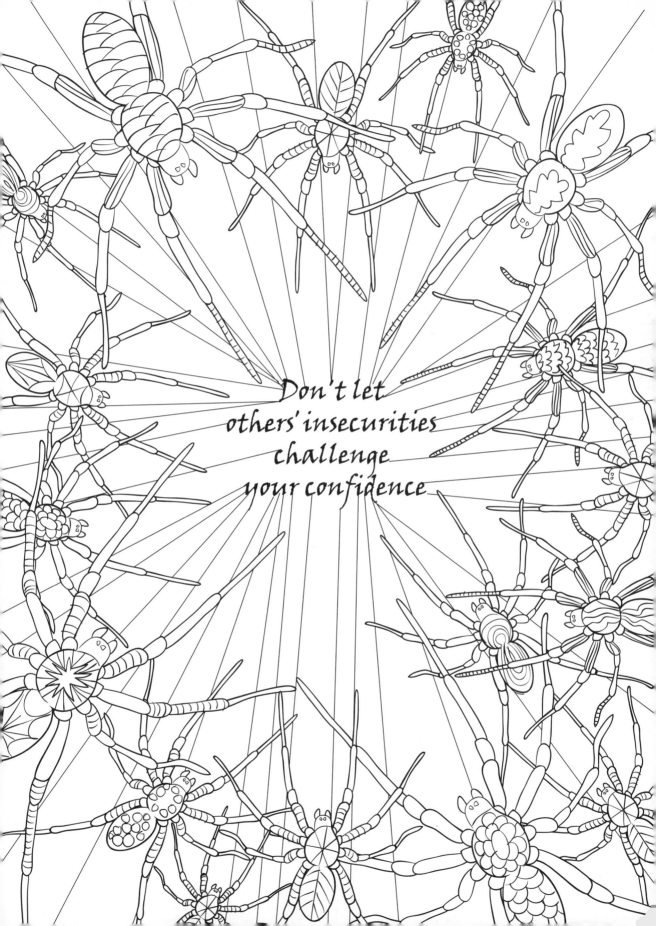

Don't let
others' insecurities
challenge
your confidence

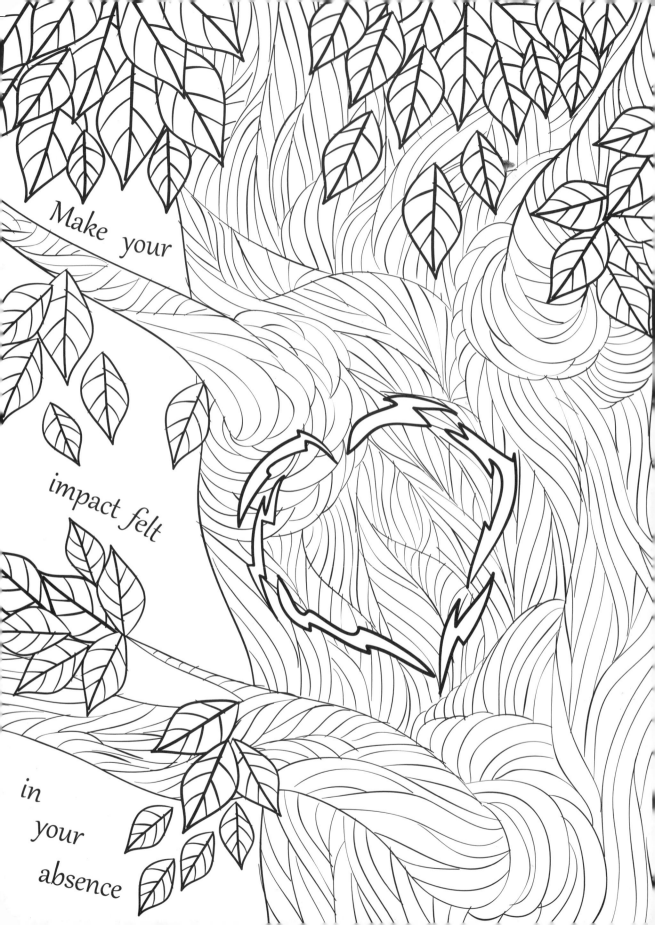

Make your

impact felt

in

your

absence

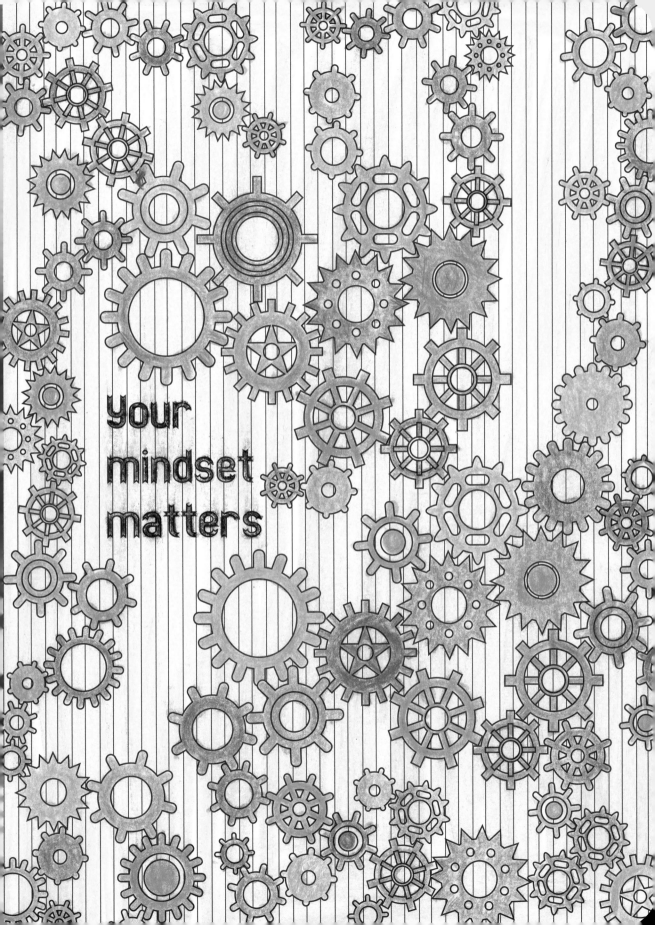

your
mindset
matters

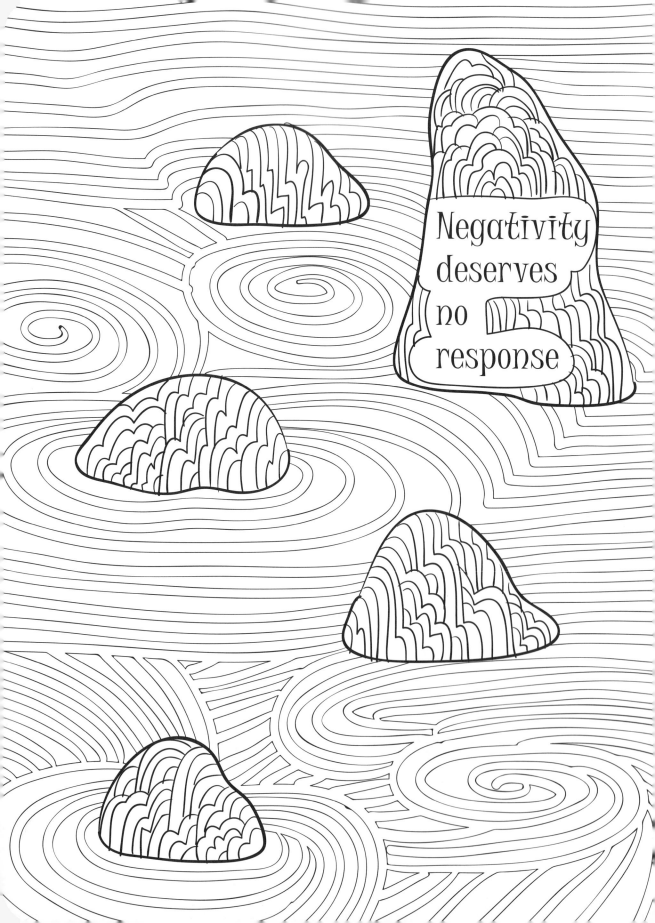

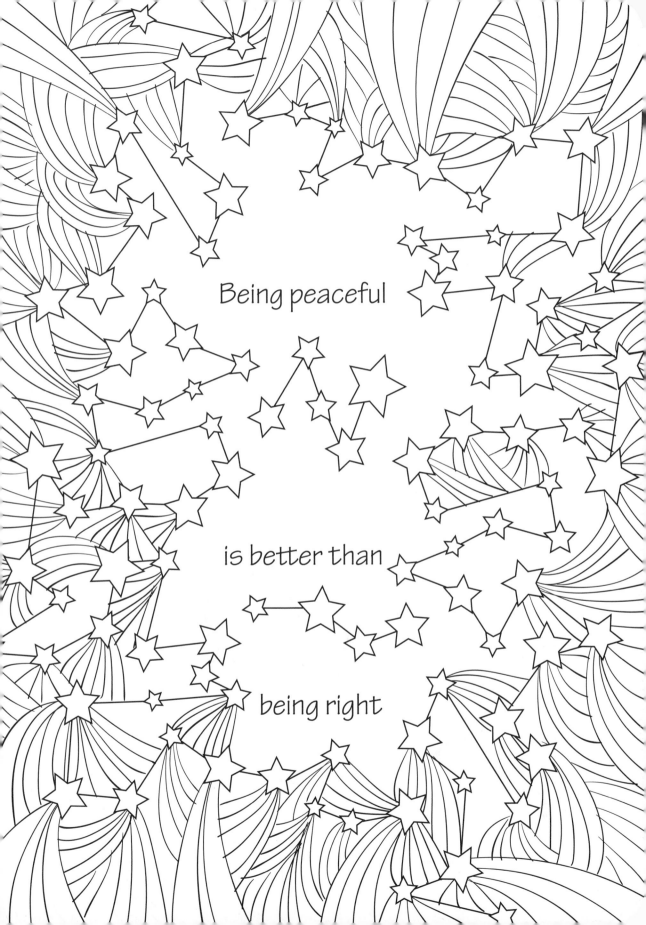

Being peaceful

is better than

being right

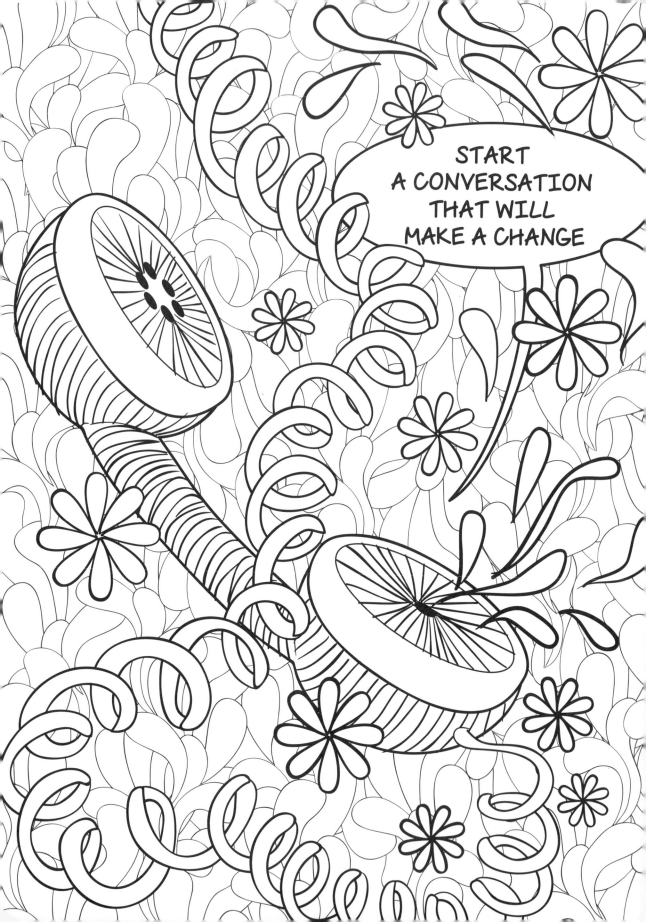

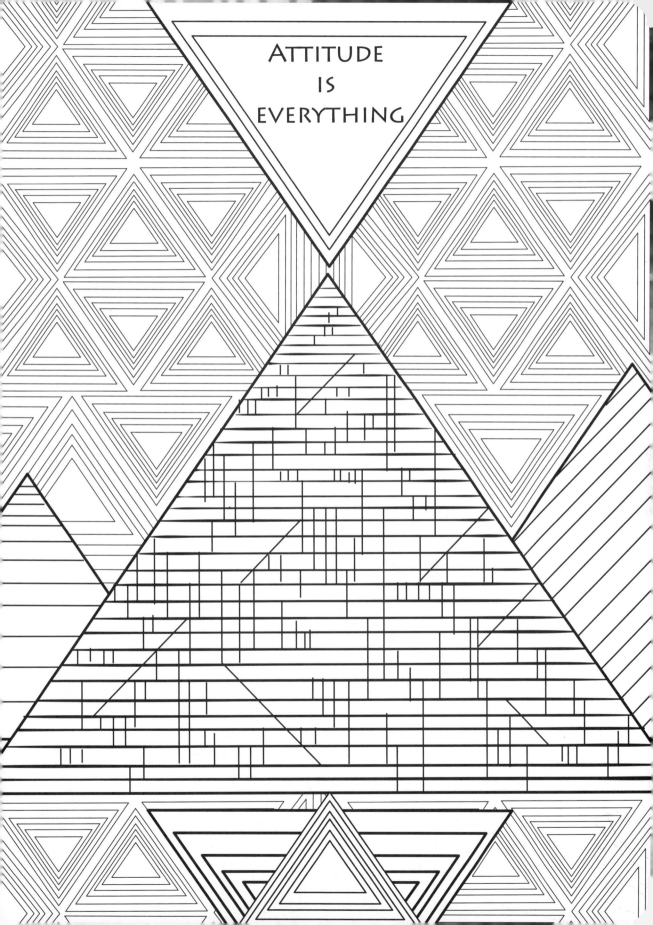

ATTITUDE
IS
EVERYTHING

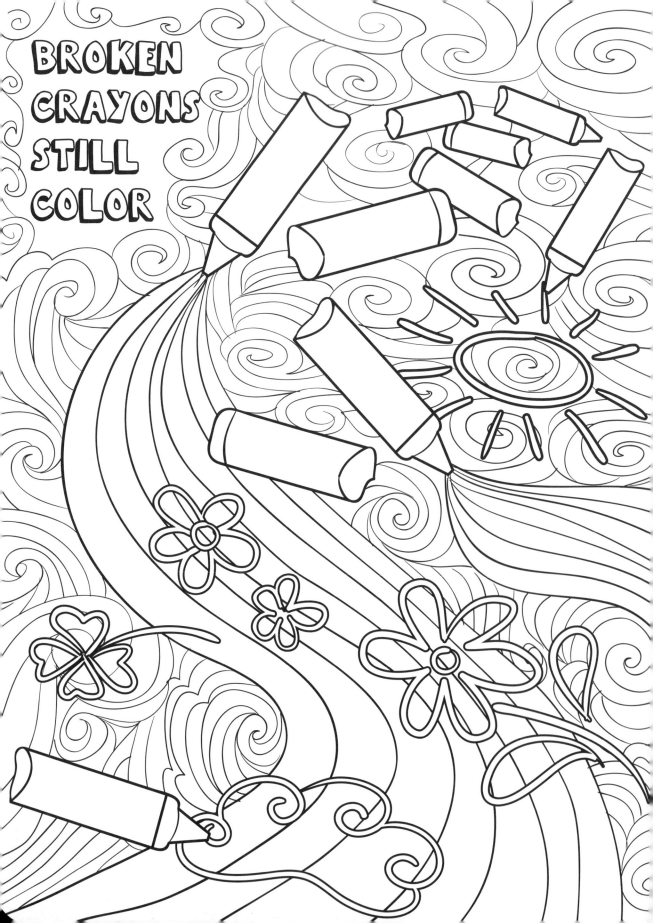

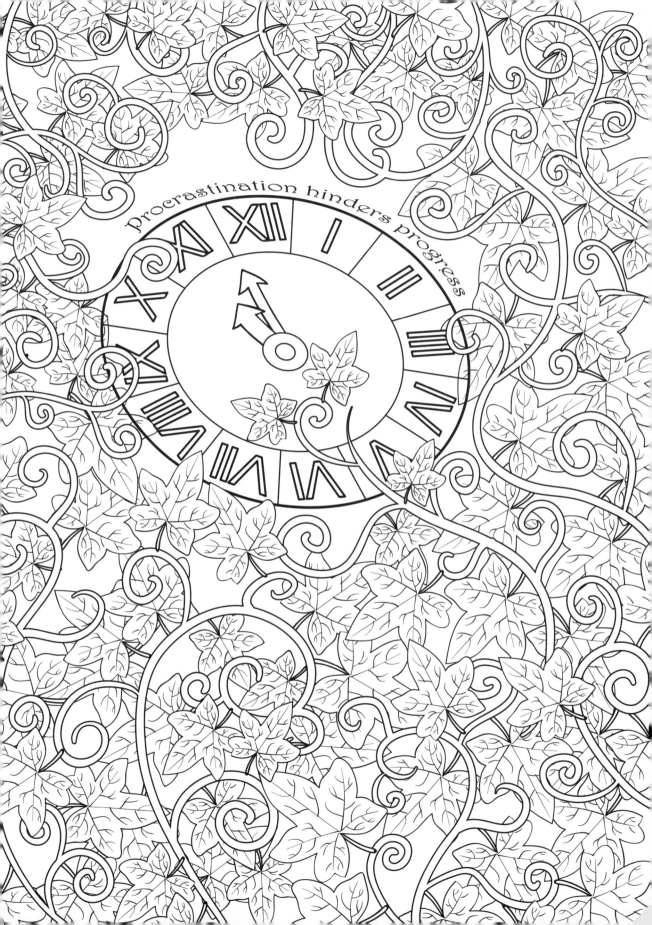

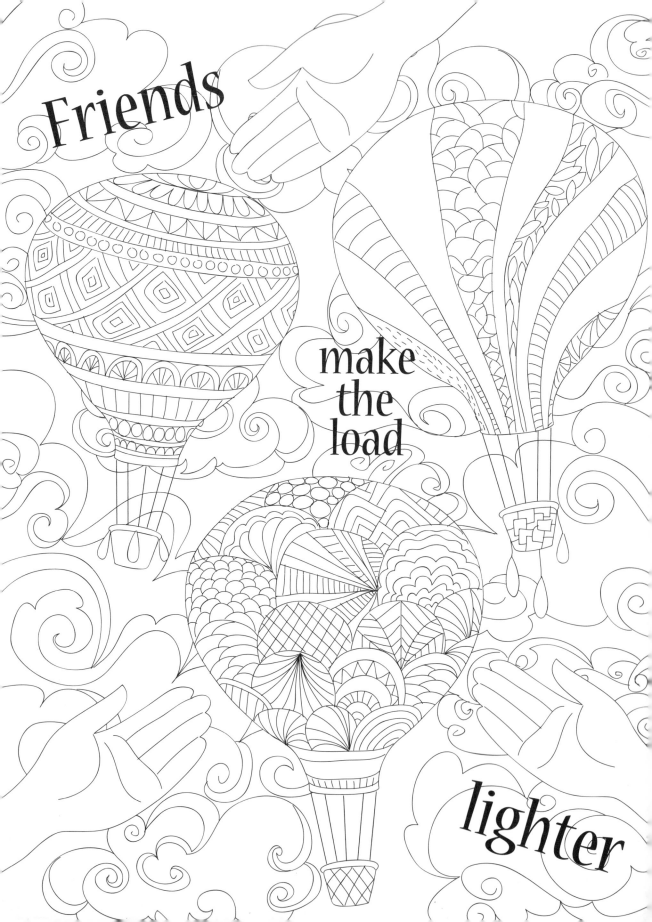

Friends

make
the
load

lighter

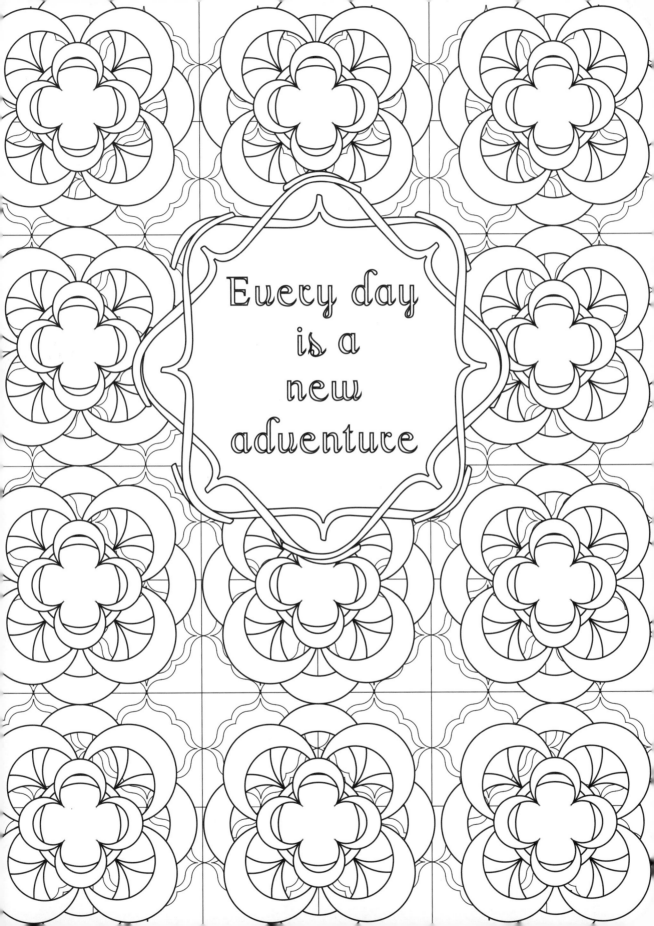

Every day
is a
new
adventure

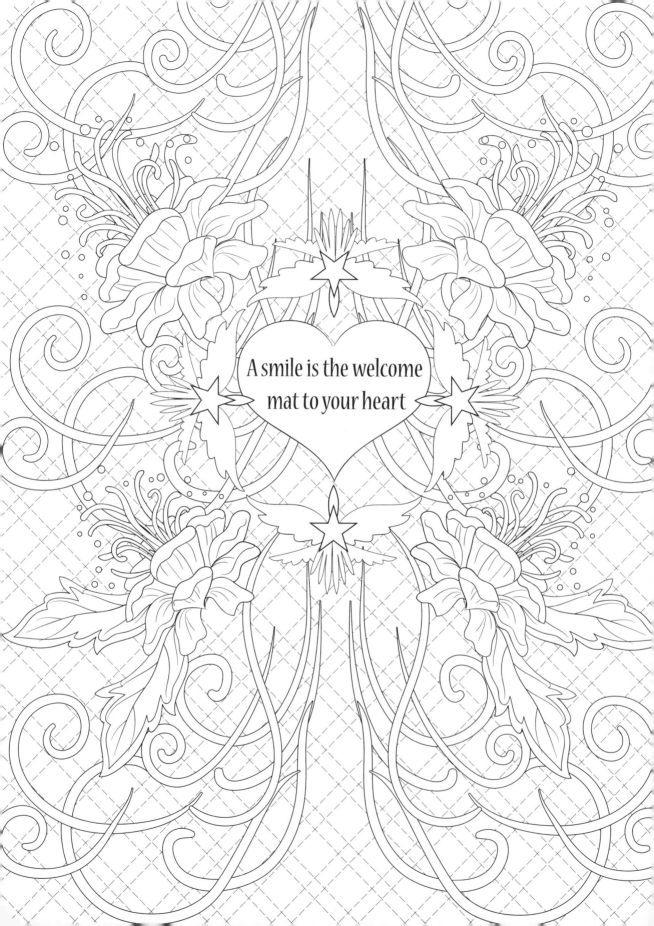

A smile is the welcome mat to your heart

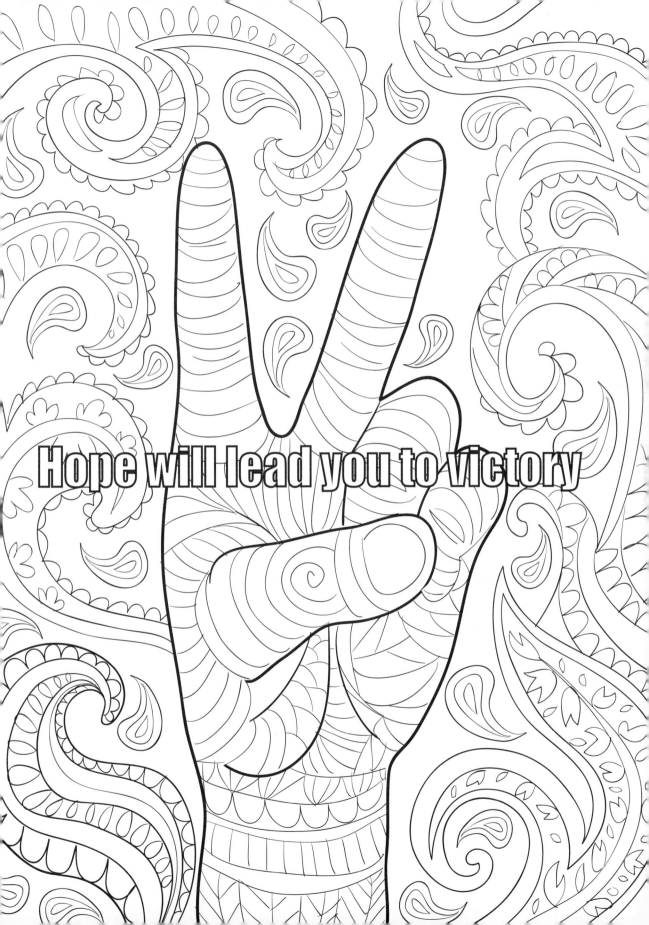

Hope will lead you to victory

Tomorrow has infinite possibilities

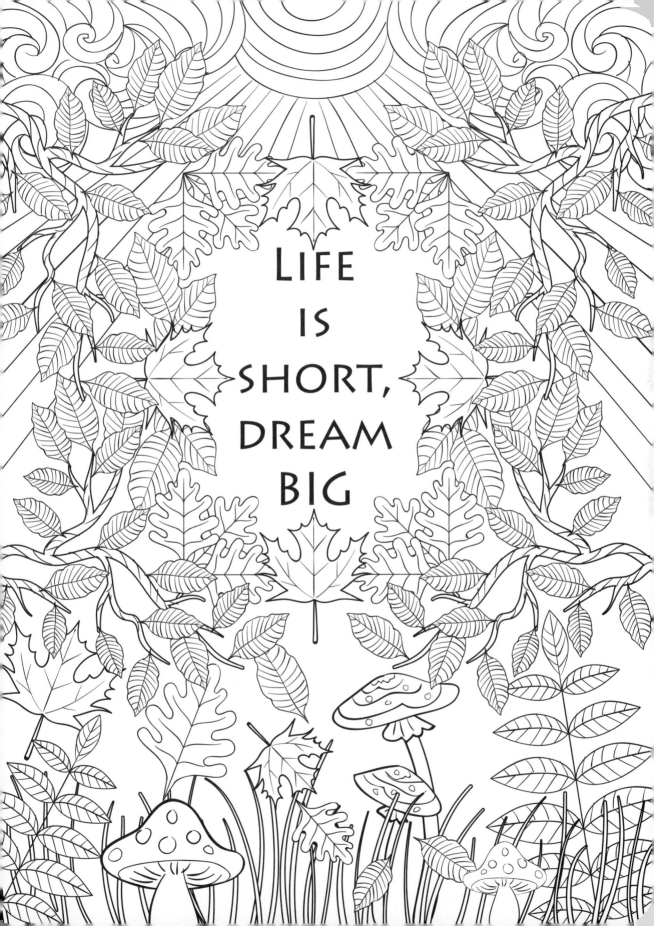

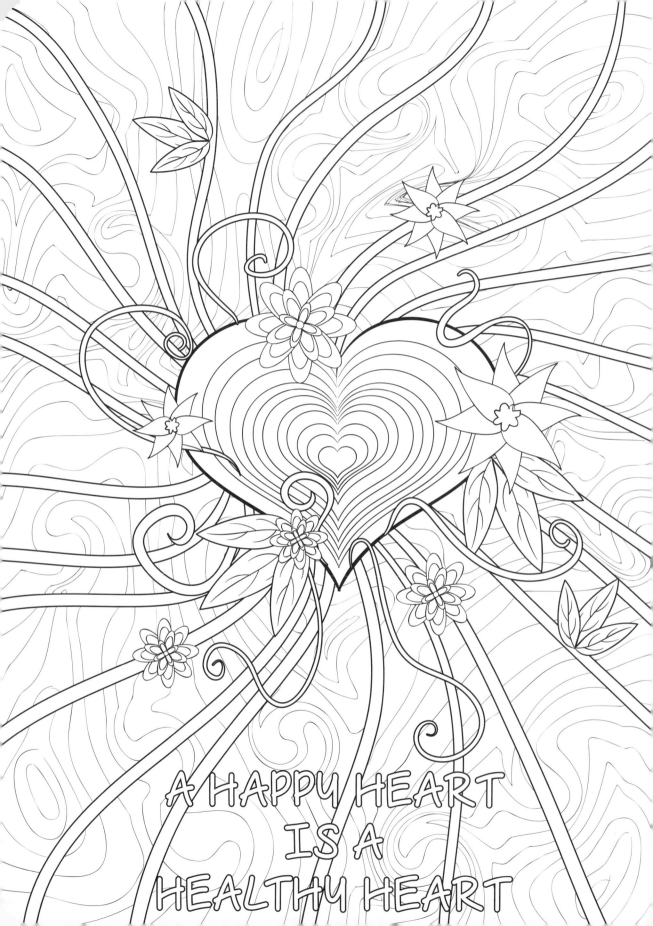

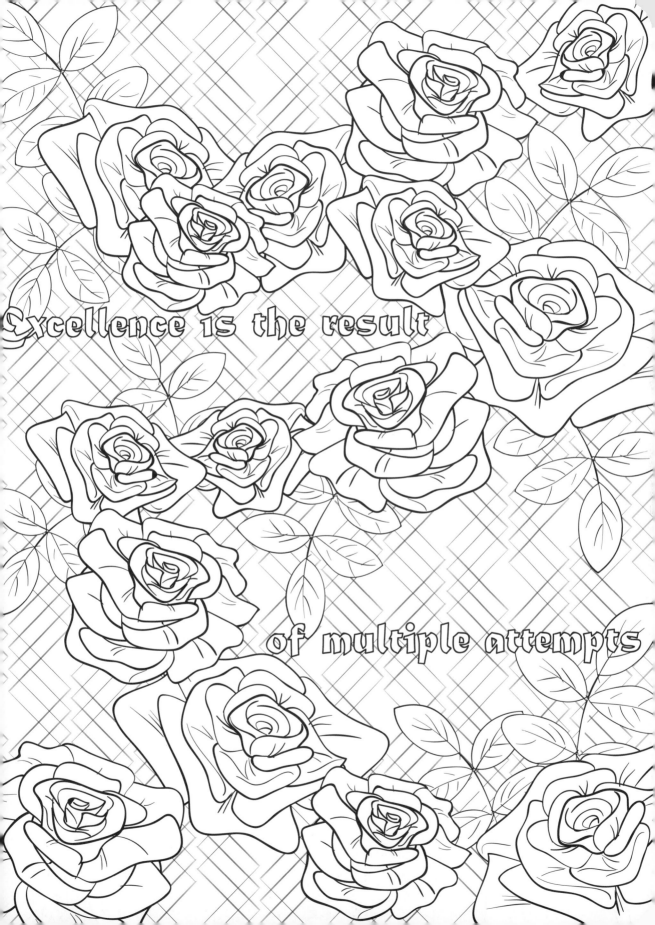

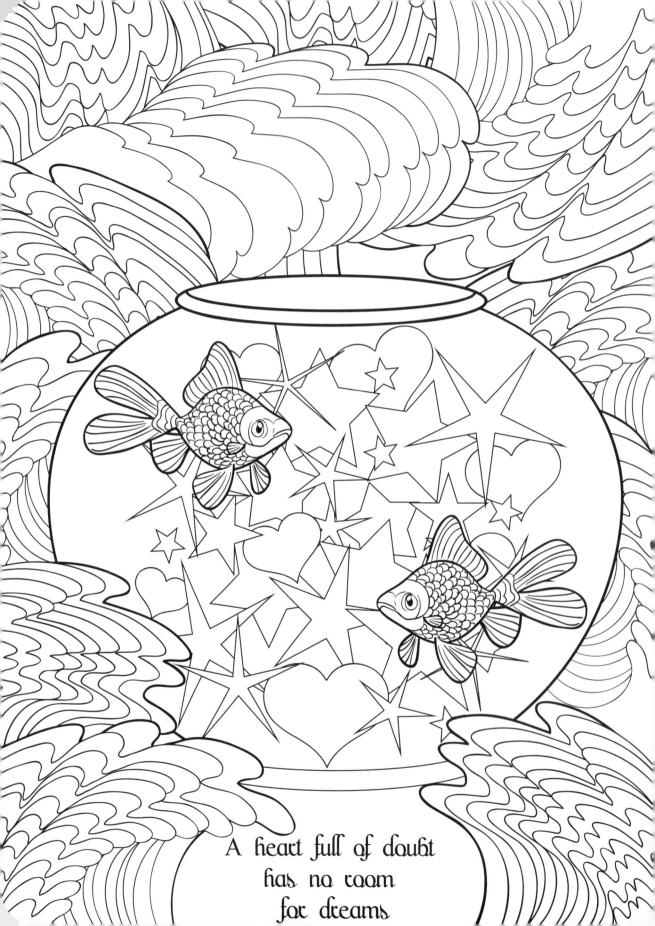

A heart full of doubt
has no room
for dreams

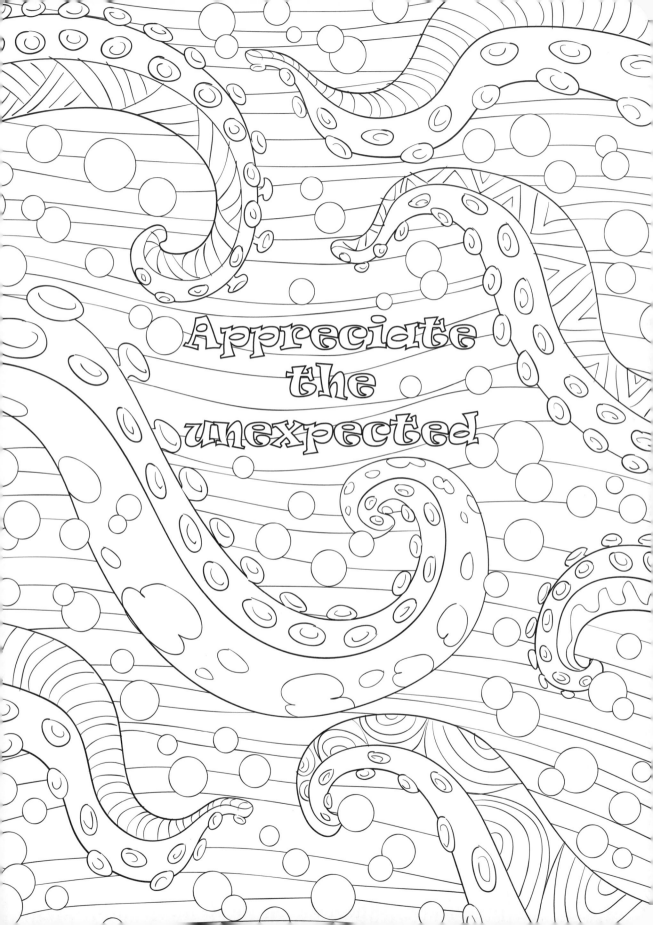

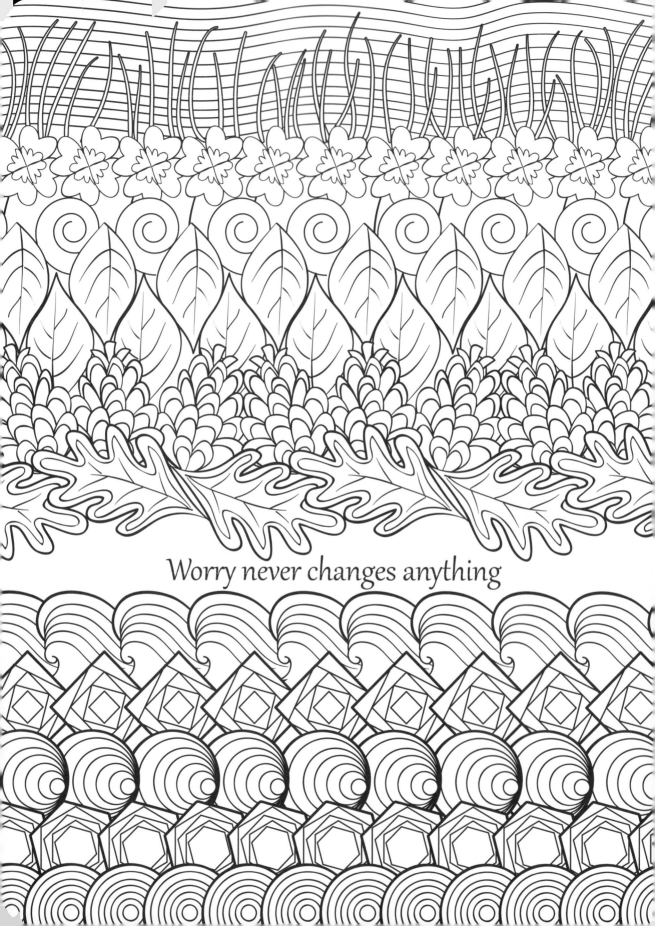

Worry never changes anything

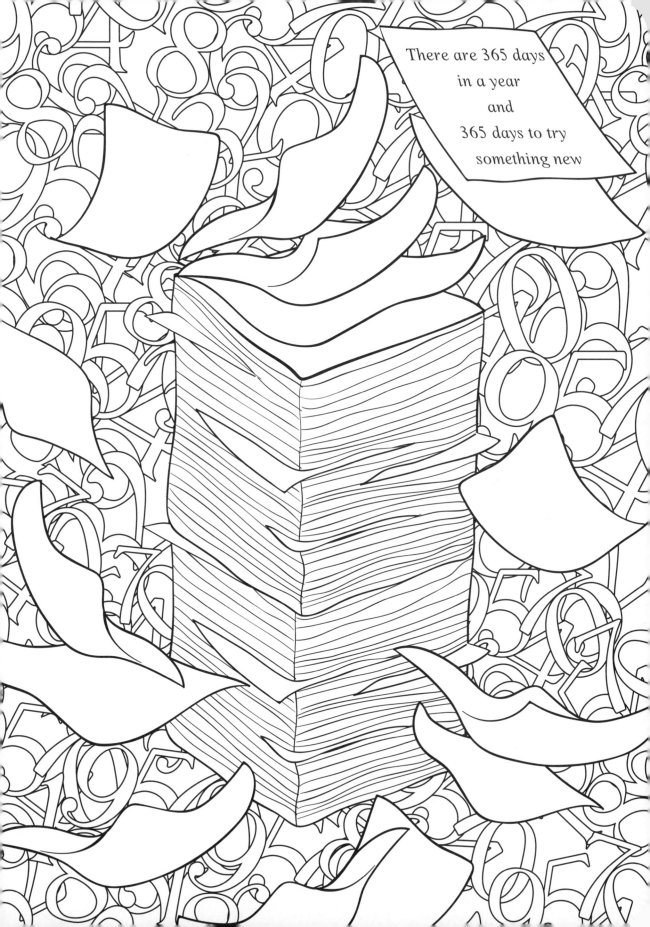

There are 365 days
in a year
and
365 days to try
something new

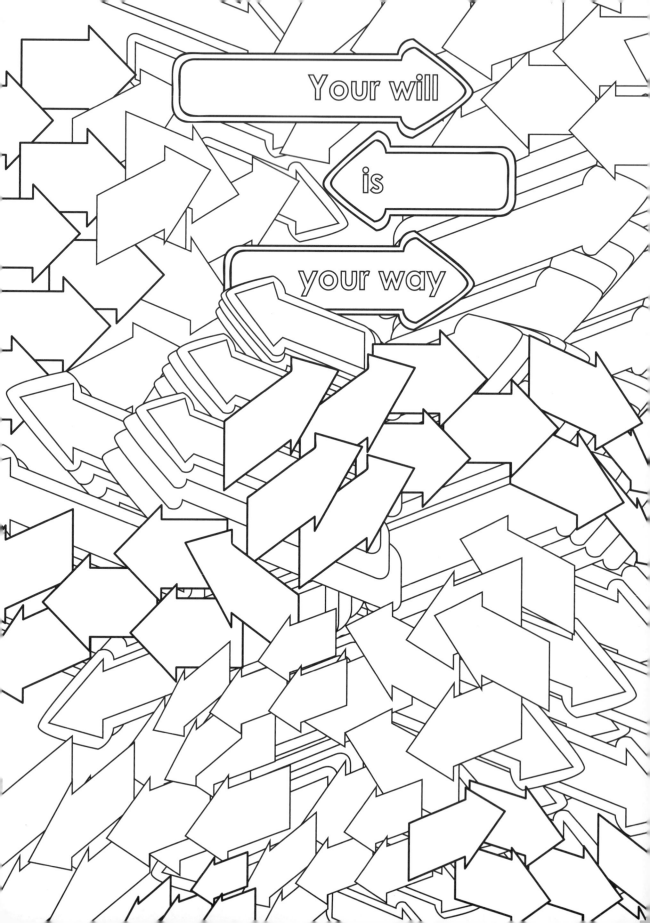

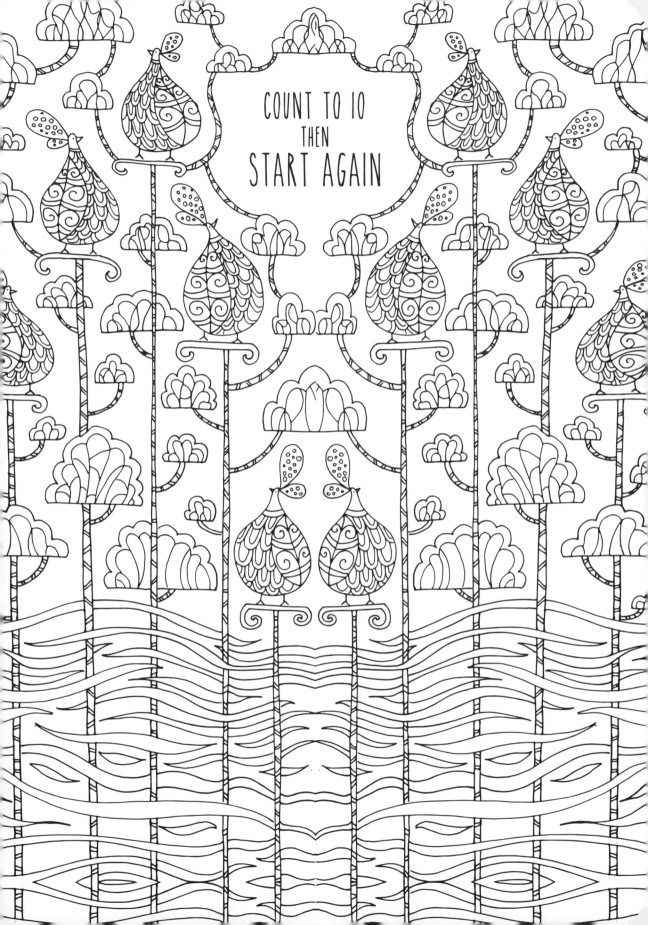

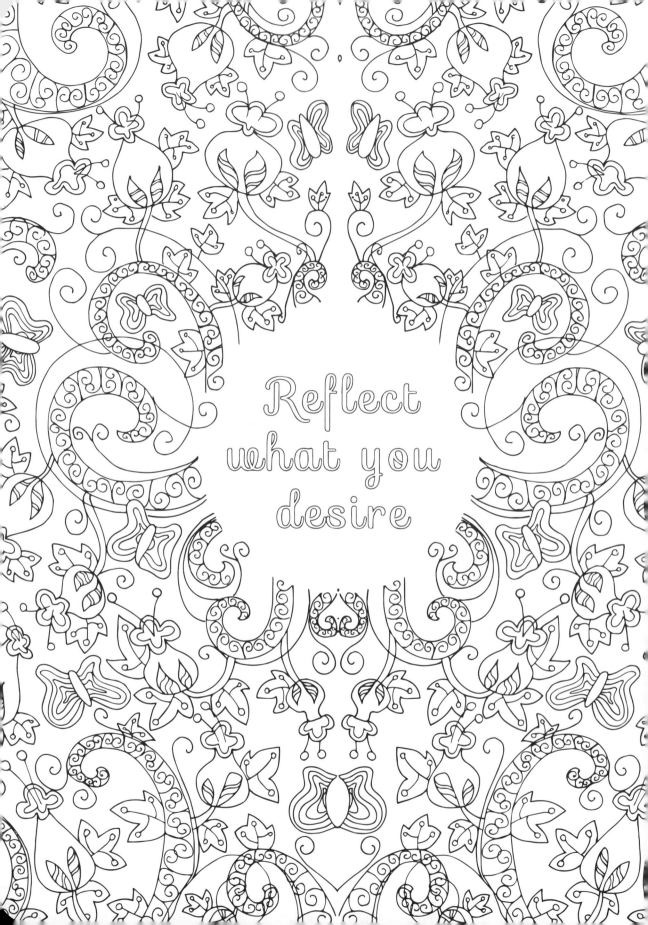

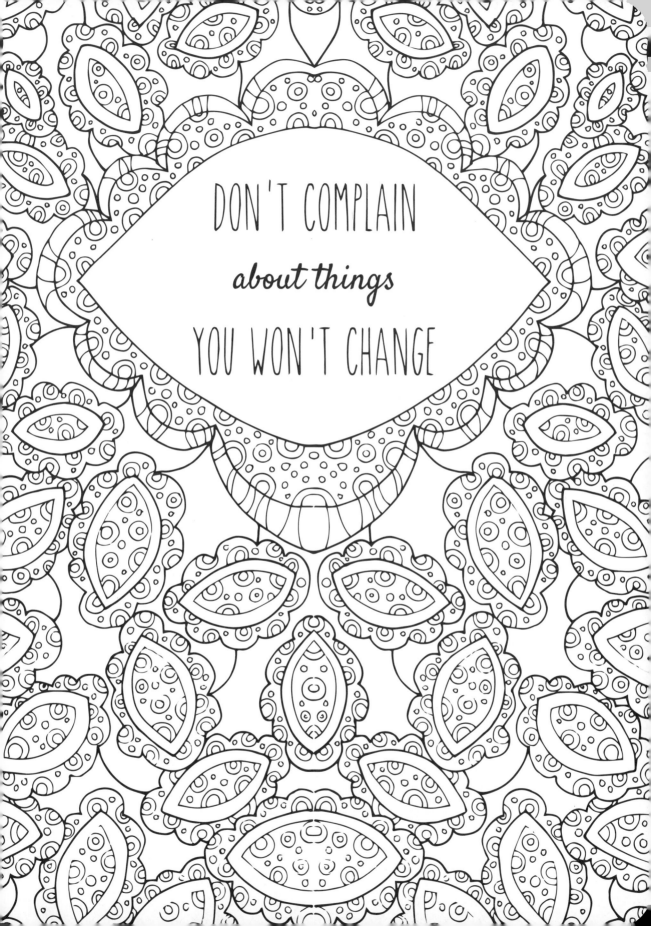

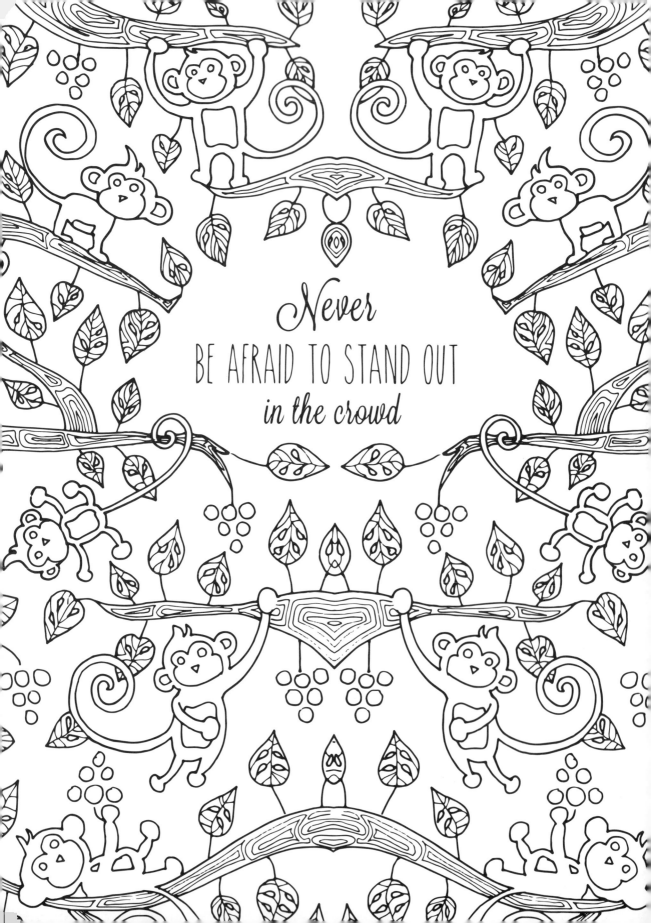

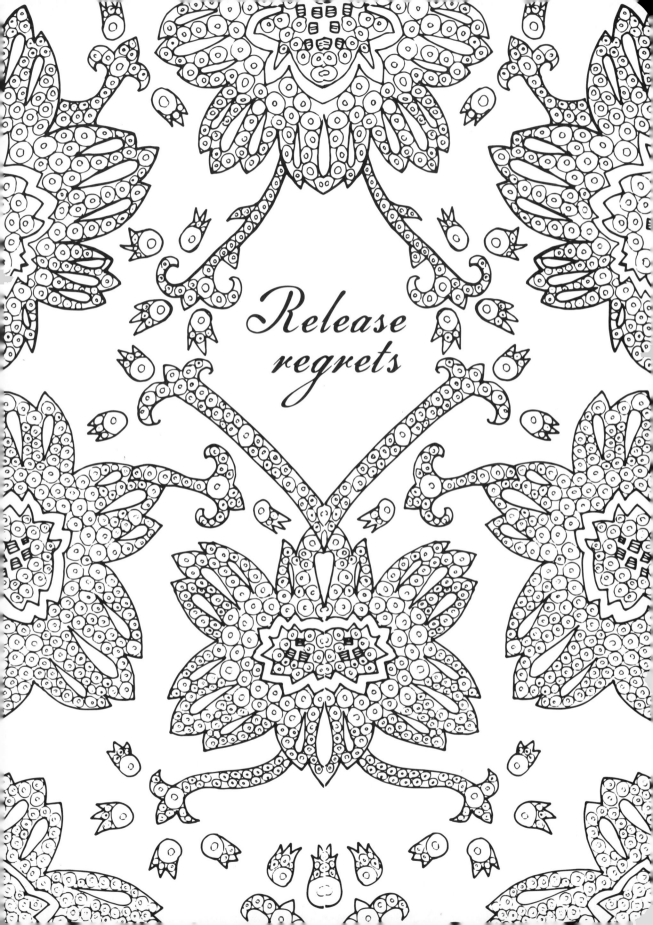

Release
regrets

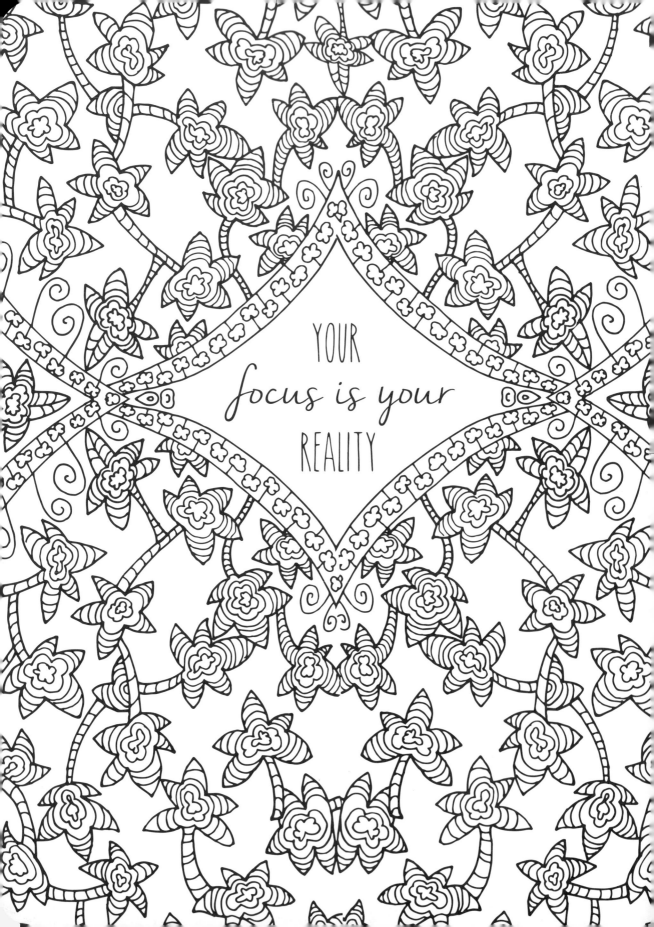

YOUR
*focus is your*
REALITY

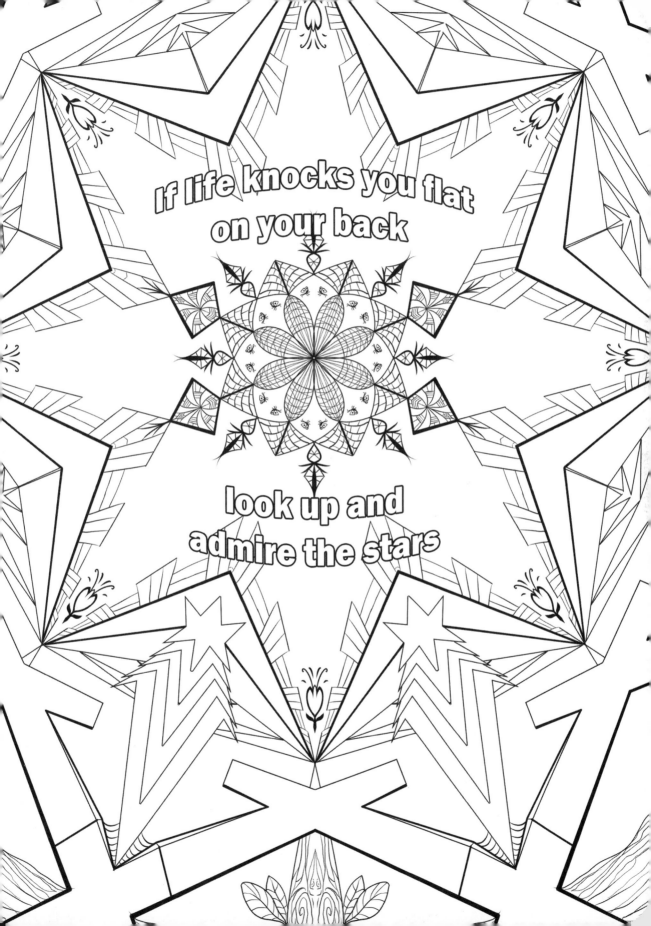

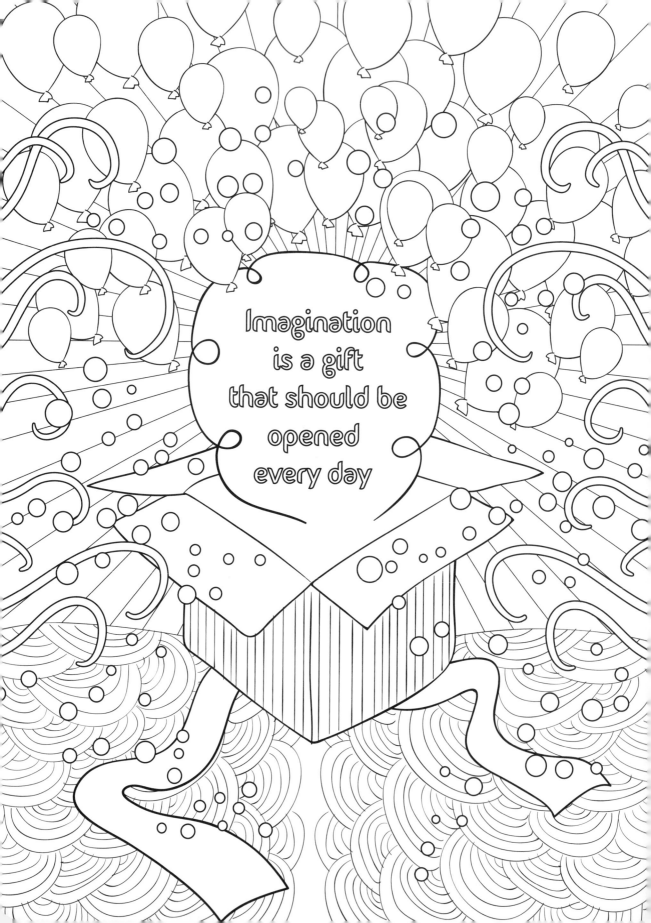

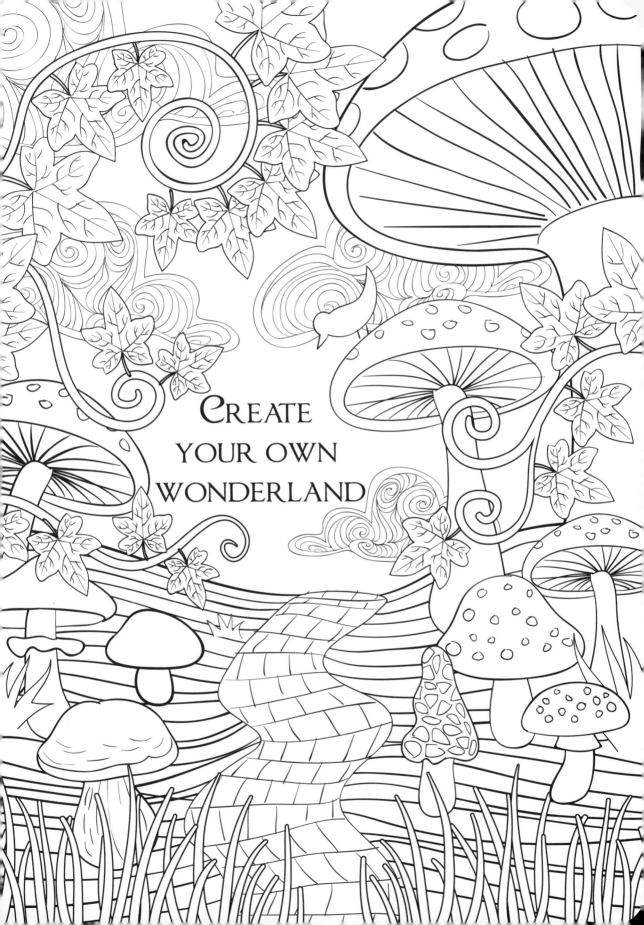

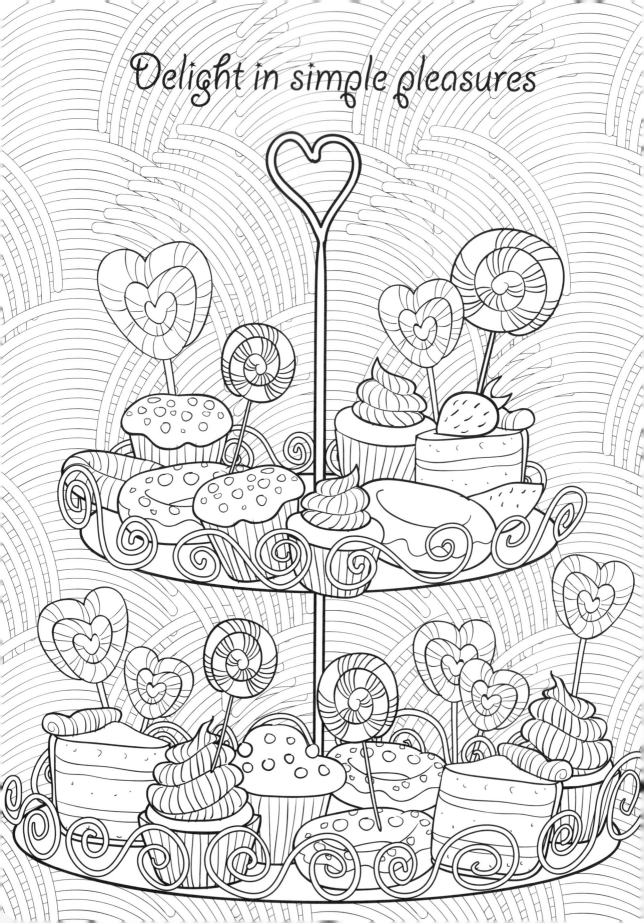

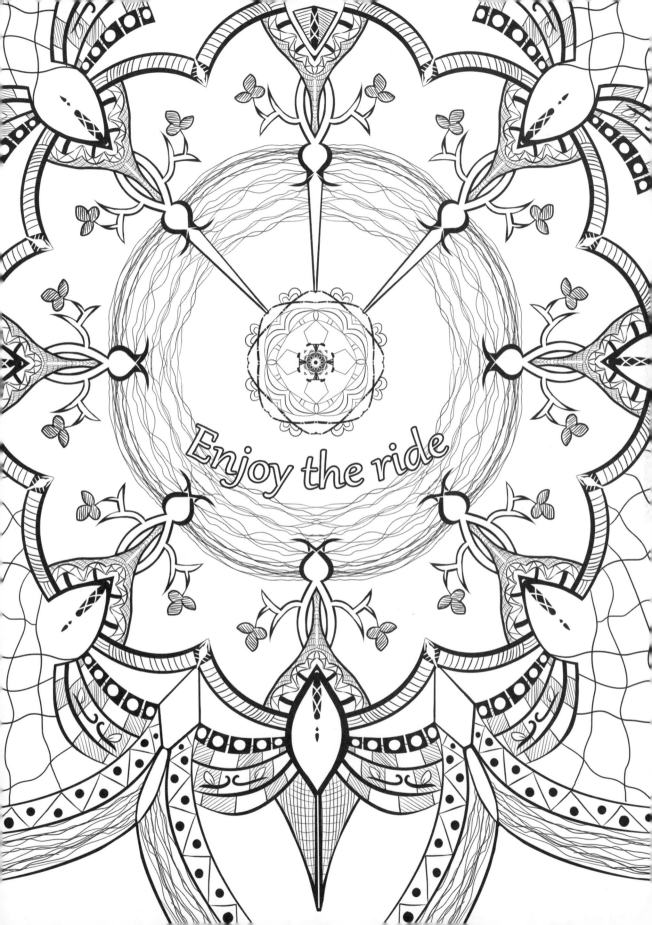

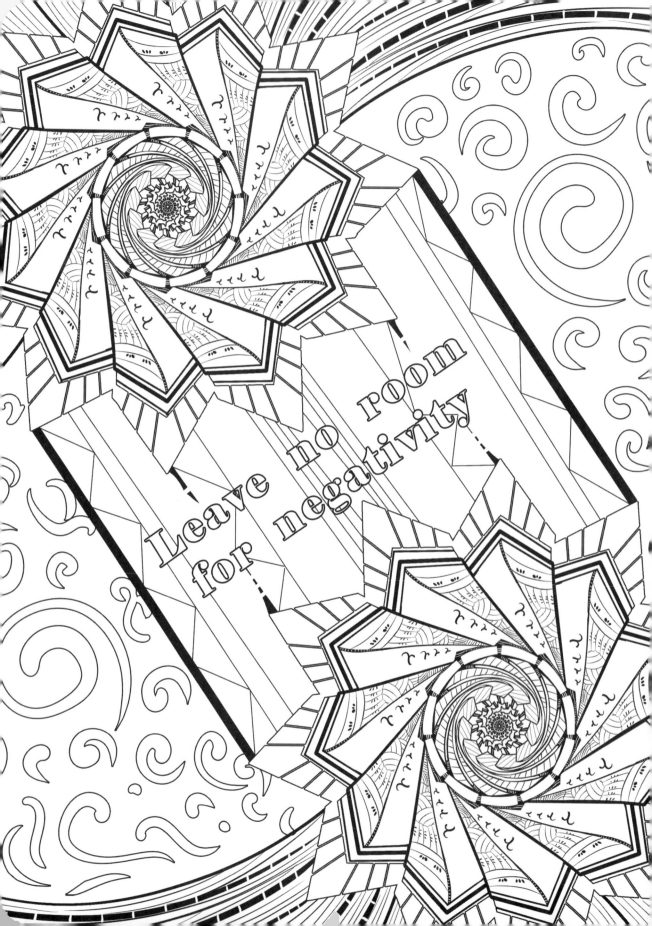

Leave no room for negativity

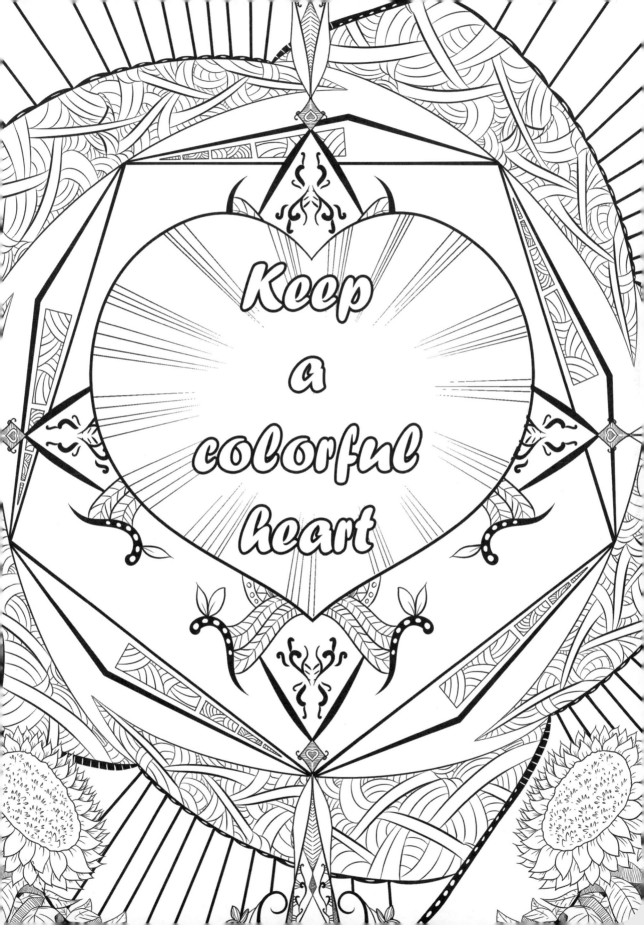

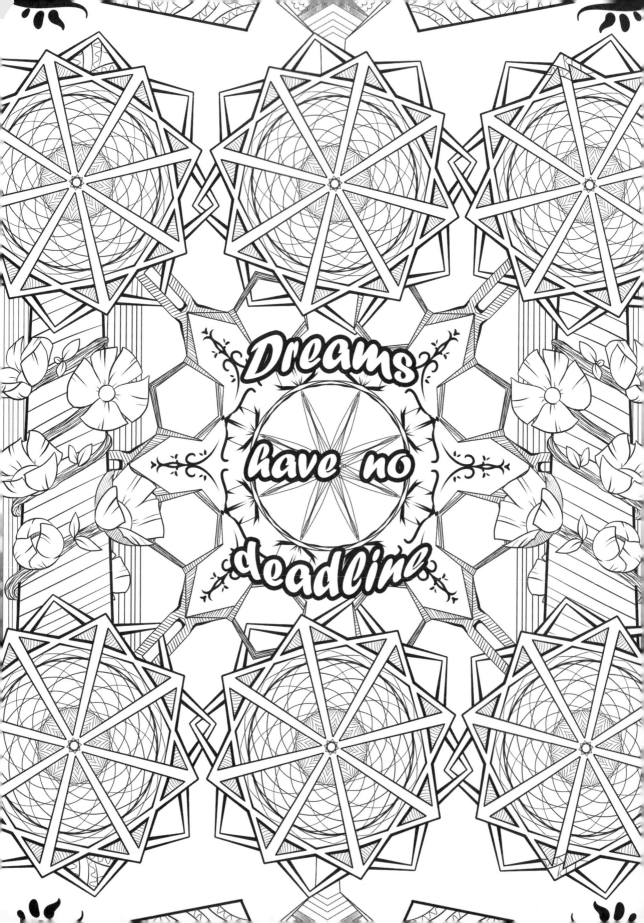

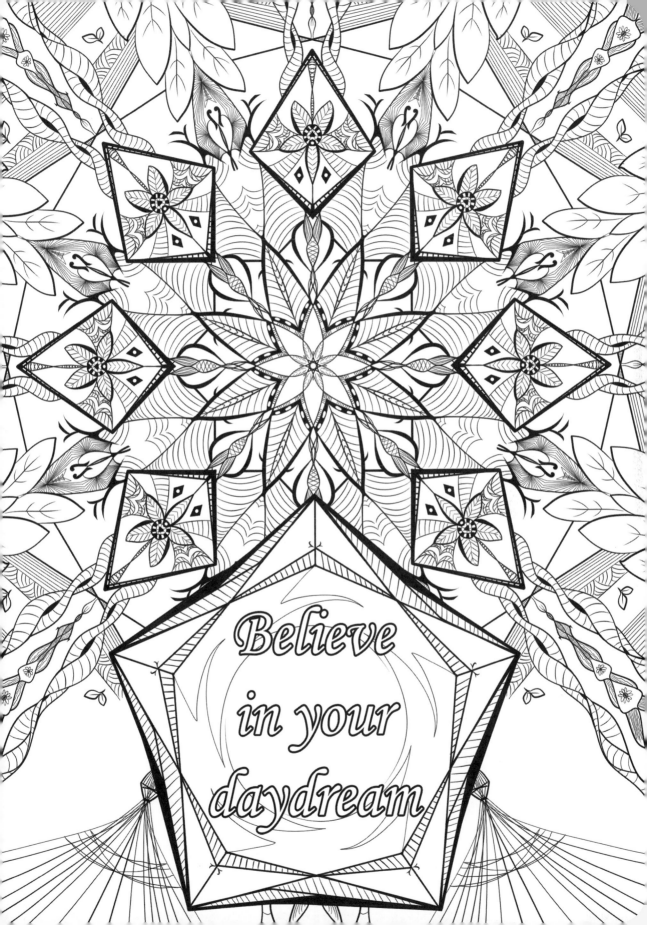

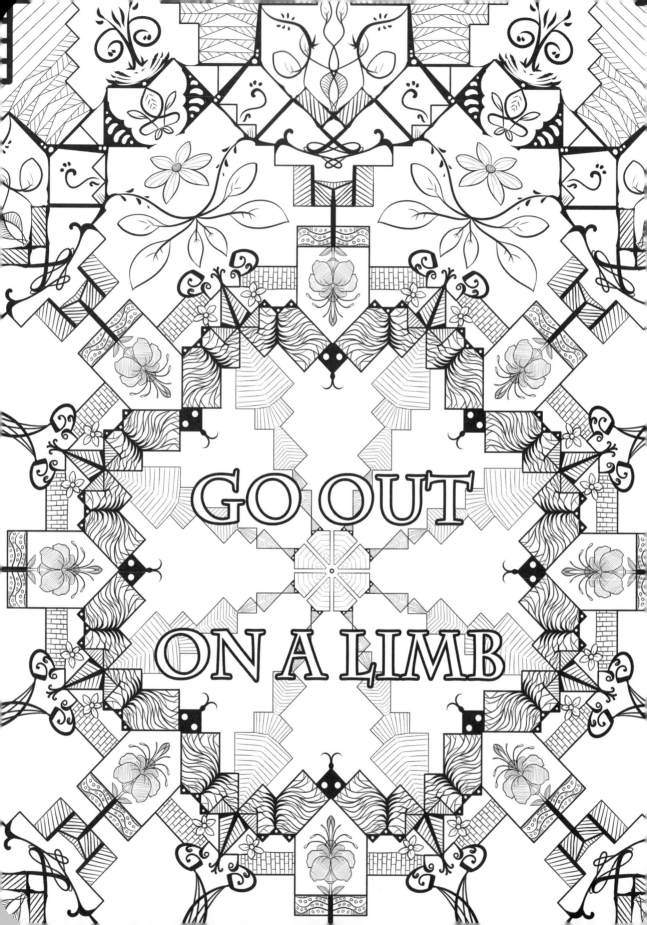

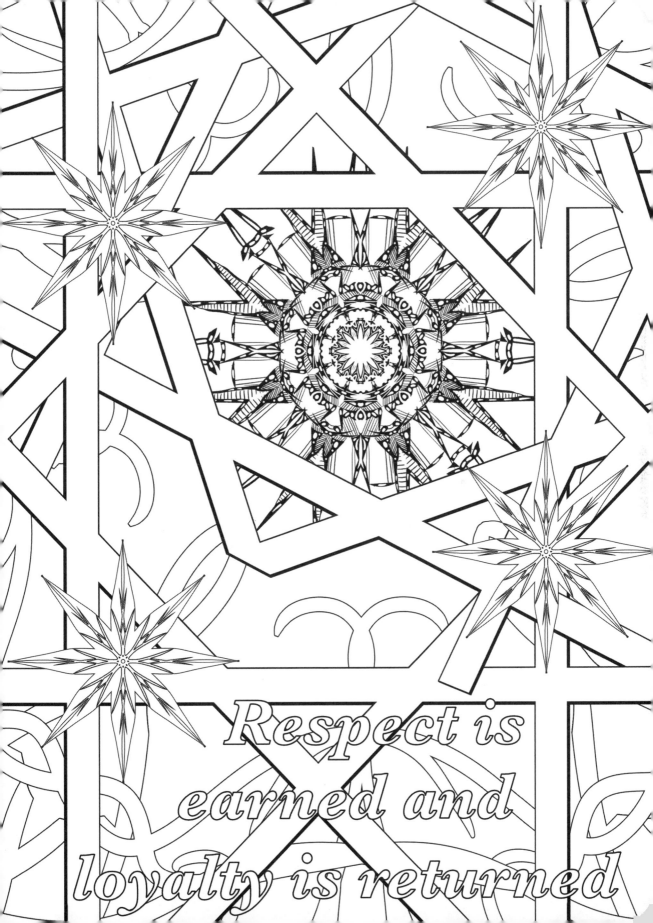

Respect is earned and loyalty is returned

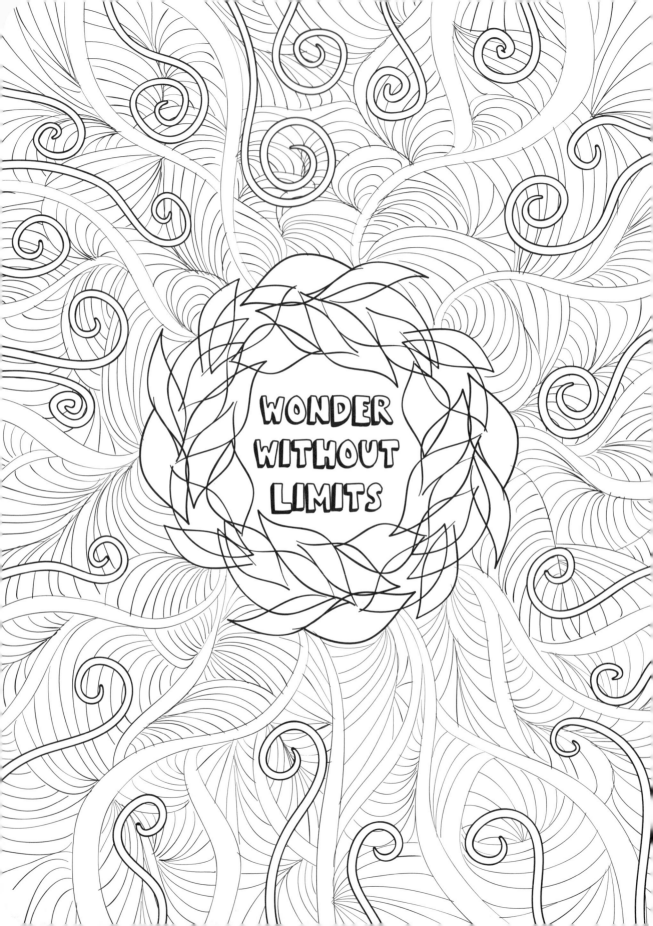

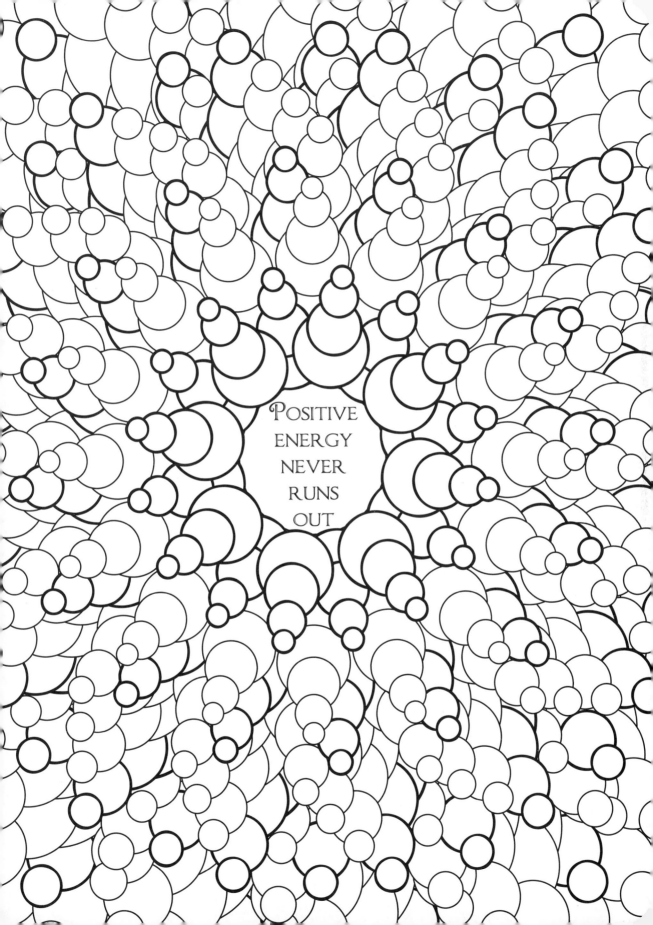

POSITIVE ENERGY NEVER RUNS OUT

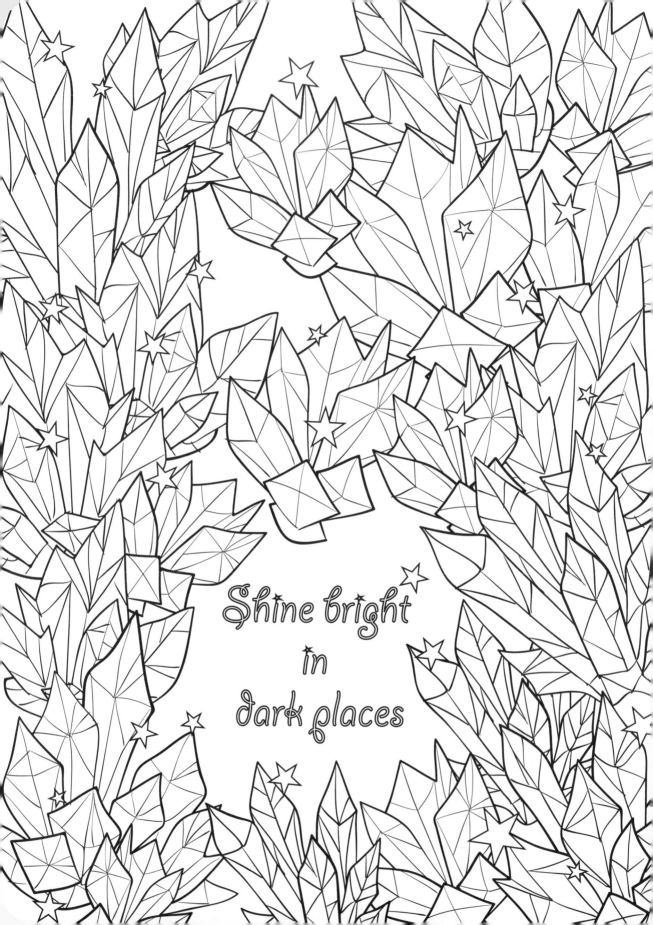

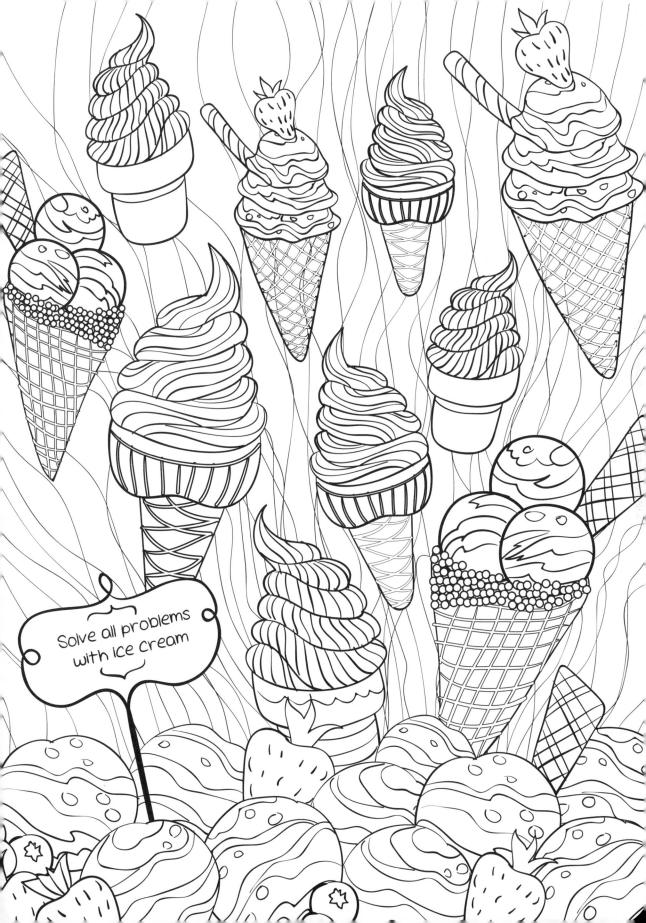

Solve all problems with ice cream

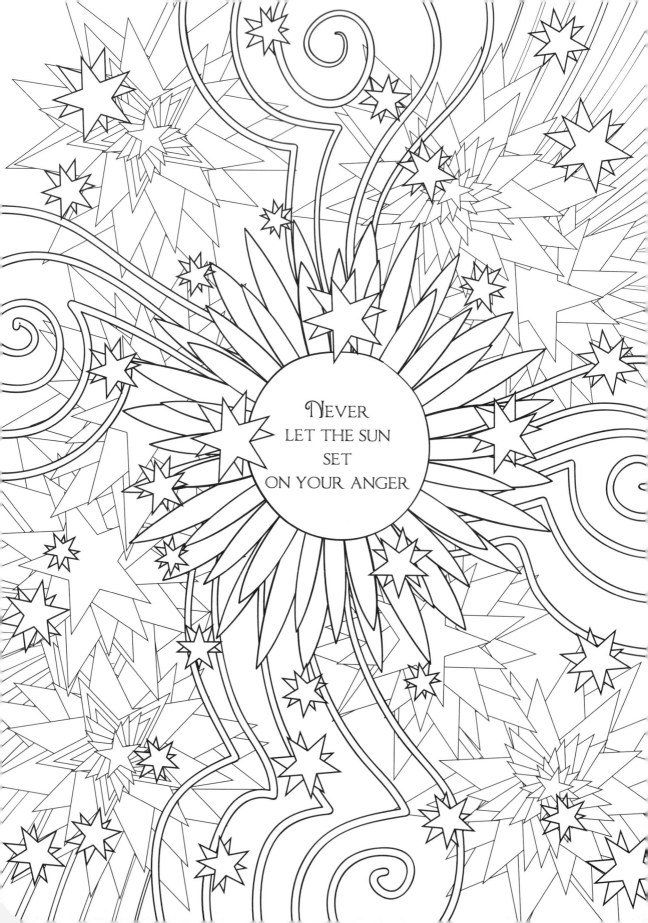

Never
let the sun
set
on your anger

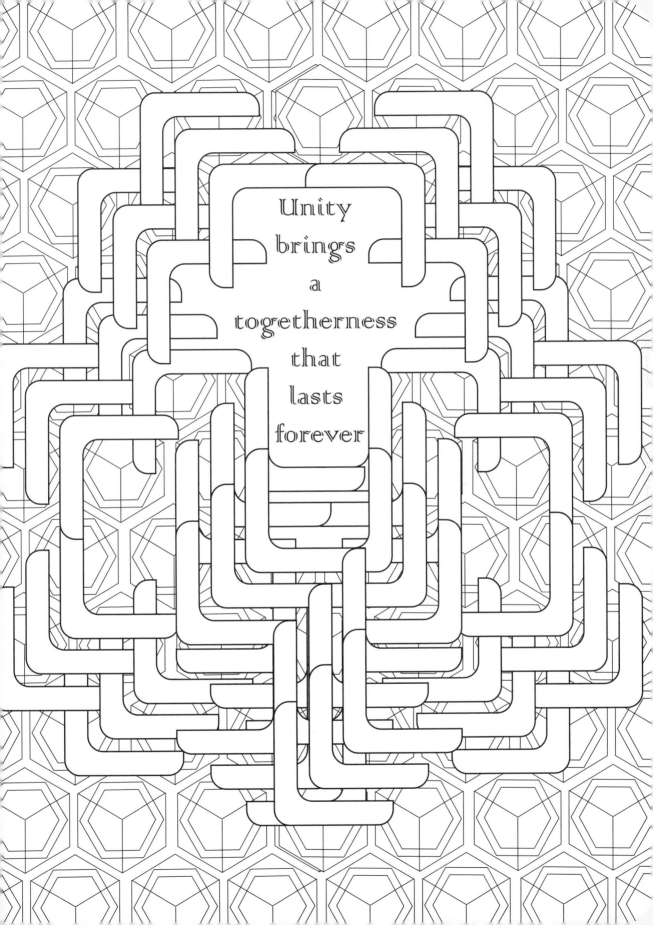

Unity
brings
a
togetherness
that
lasts
forever

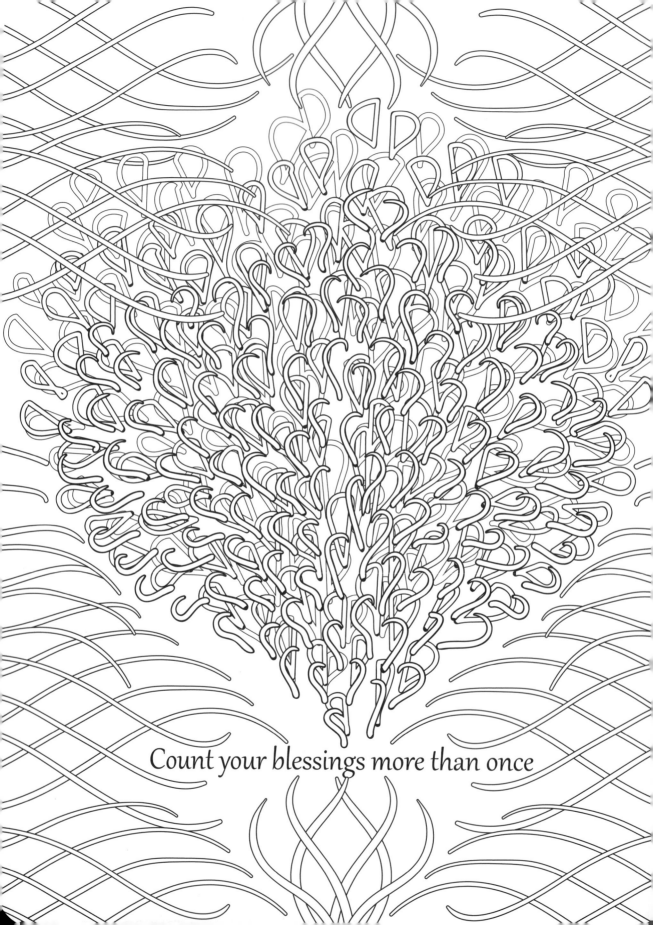

Count your blessings more than once

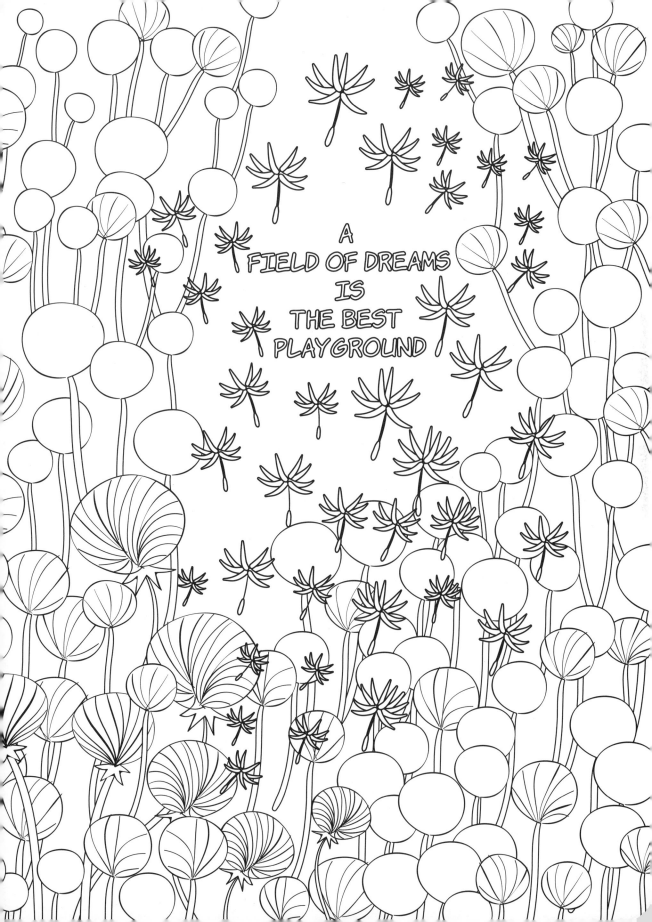

A
FIELD OF DREAMS
IS
THE BEST
PLAYGROUND

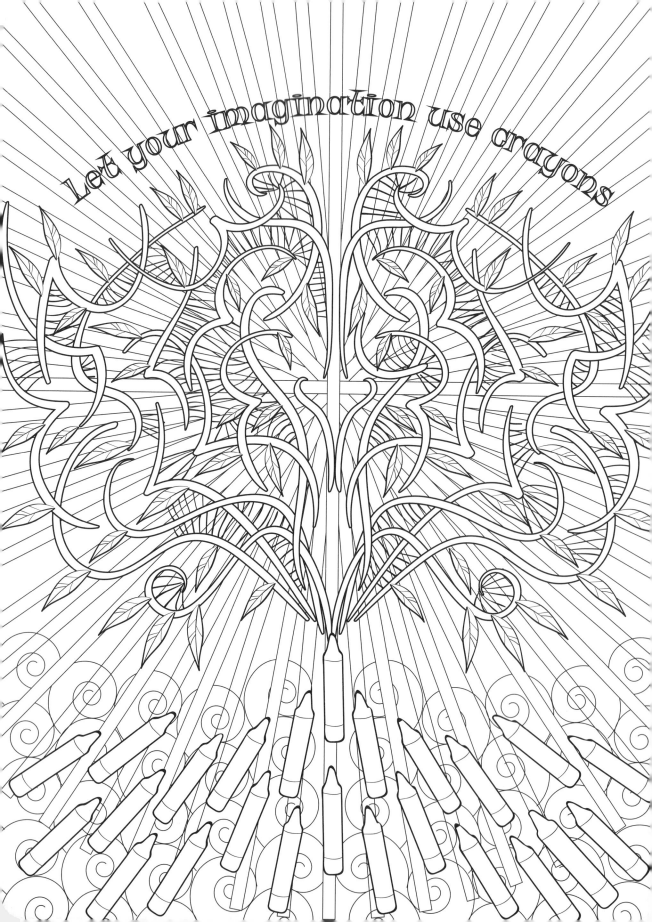

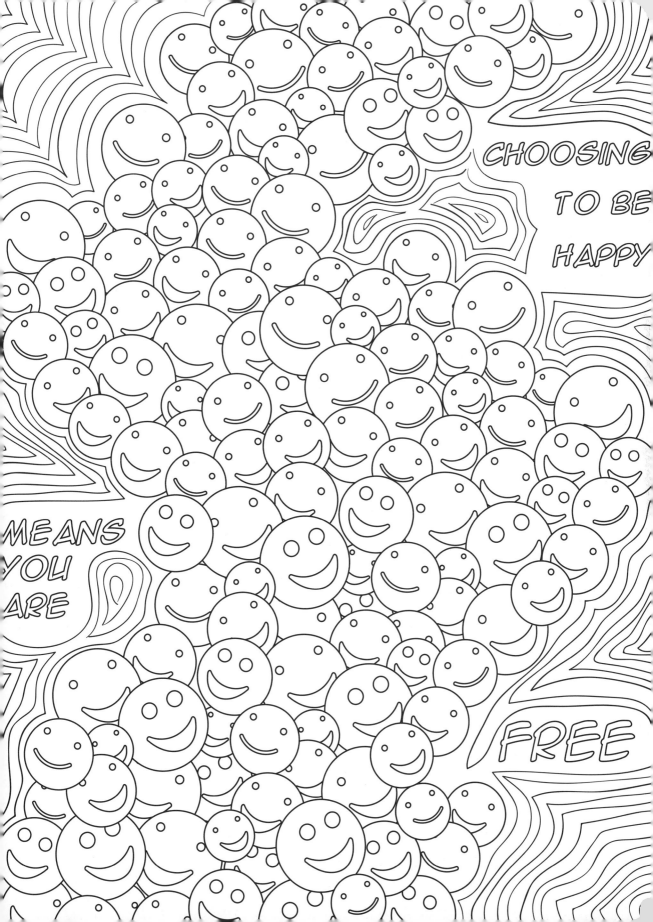

CHOOSING TO BE HAPPY MEANS YOU ARE FREE

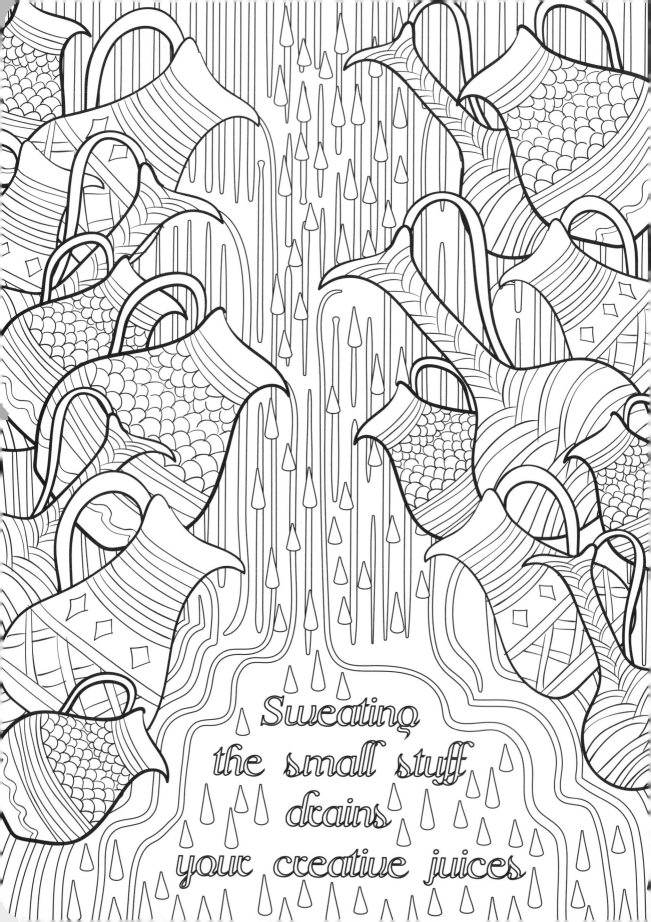

Sweating
the small stuff
drains
your creative juices

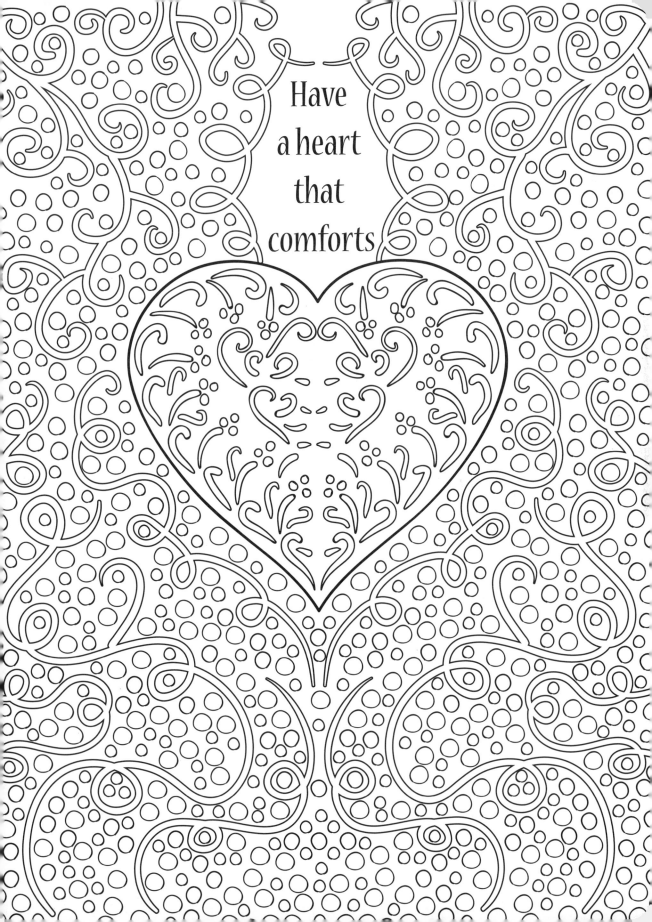

Have
a heart
that
comforts

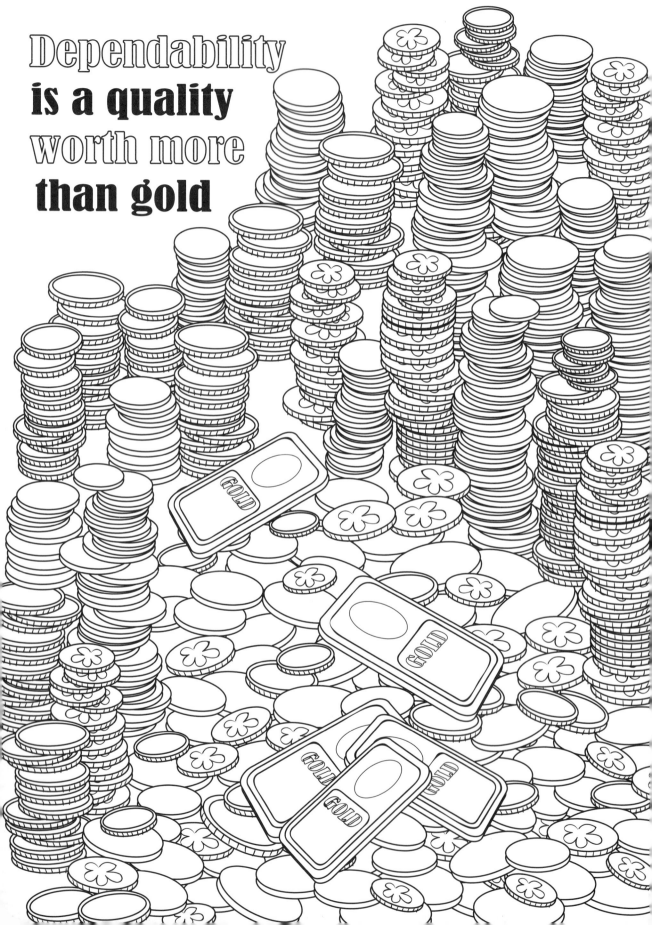

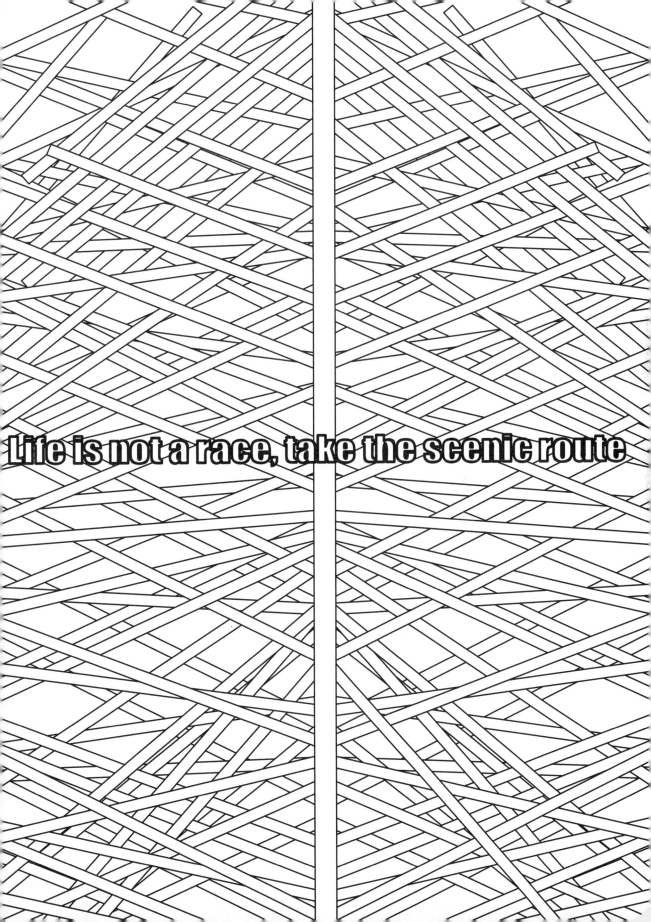

Life is not a race, take the scenic route

Don't just stop
and smell the roses,
plant some

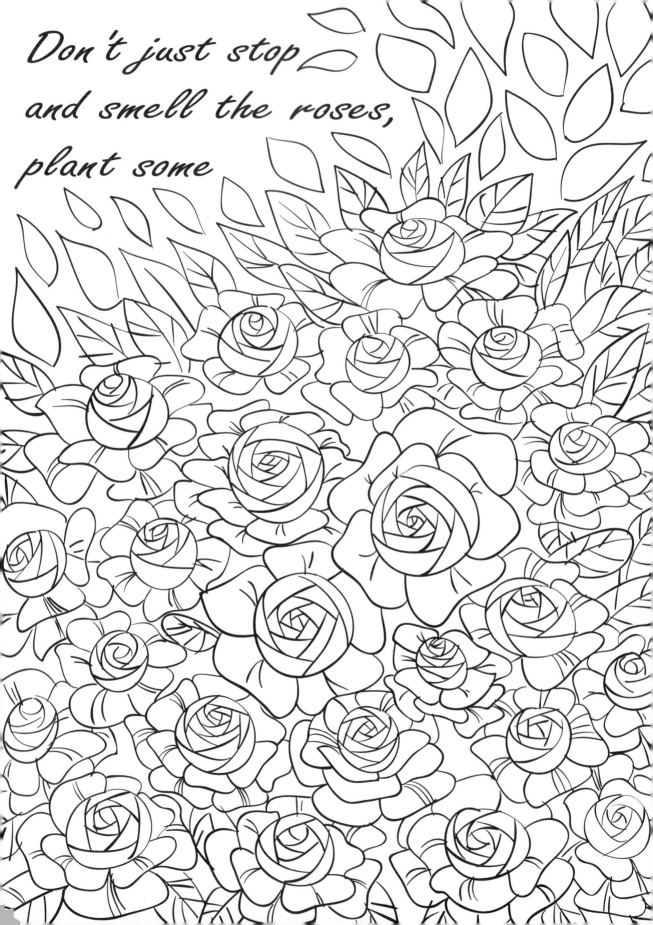

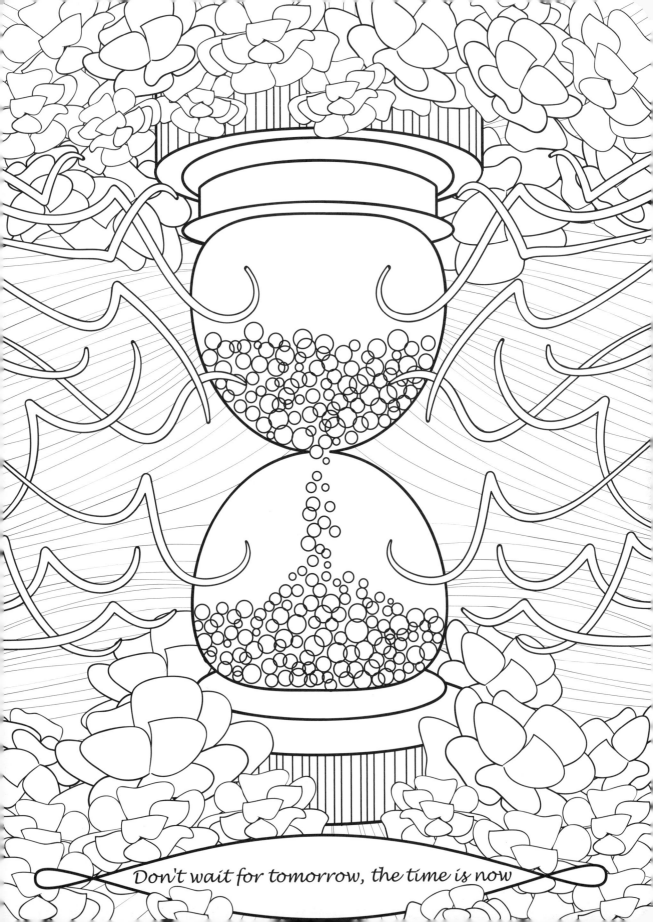

Don't wait for tomorrow, the time is now

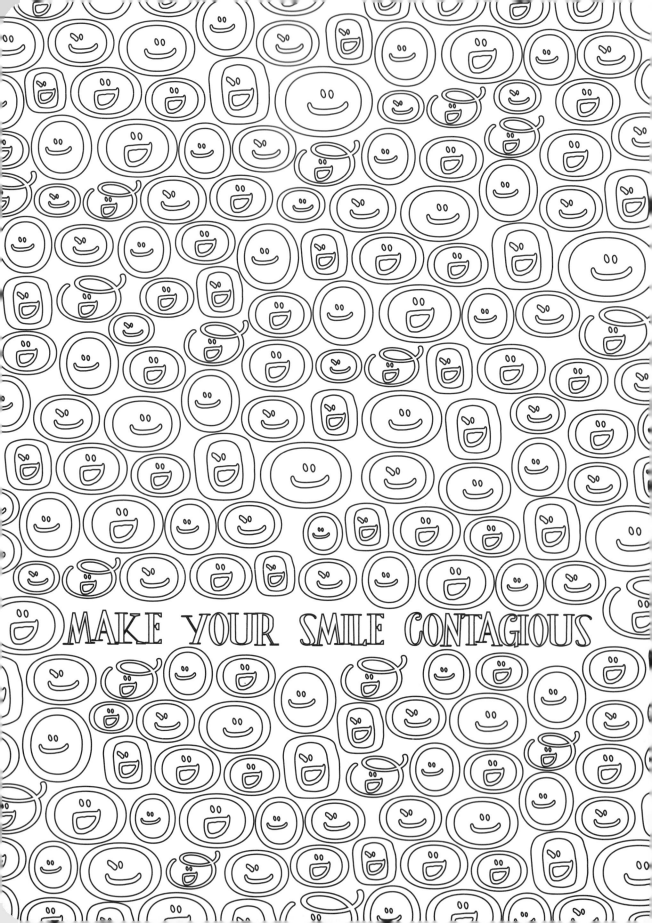

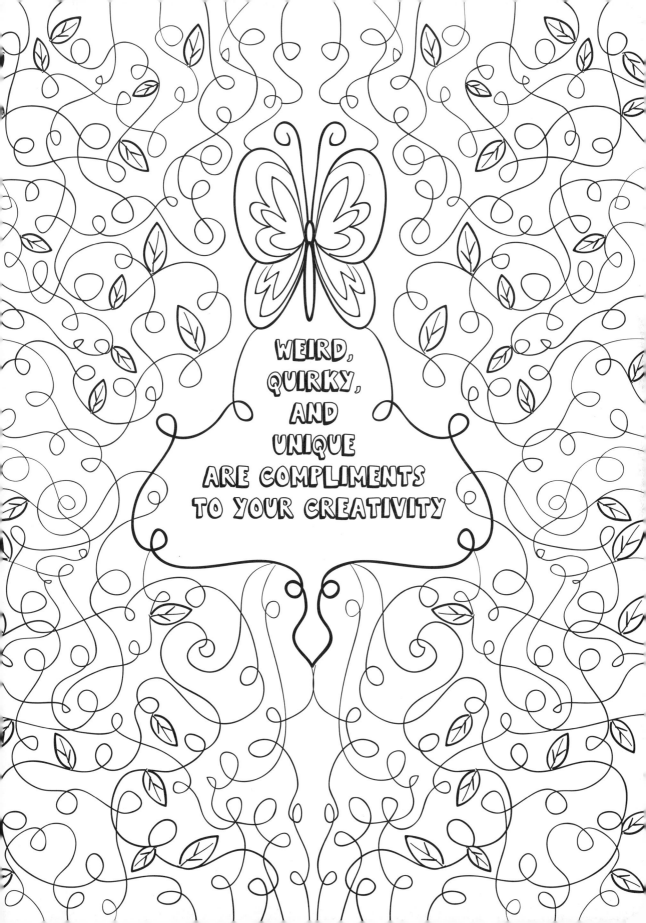

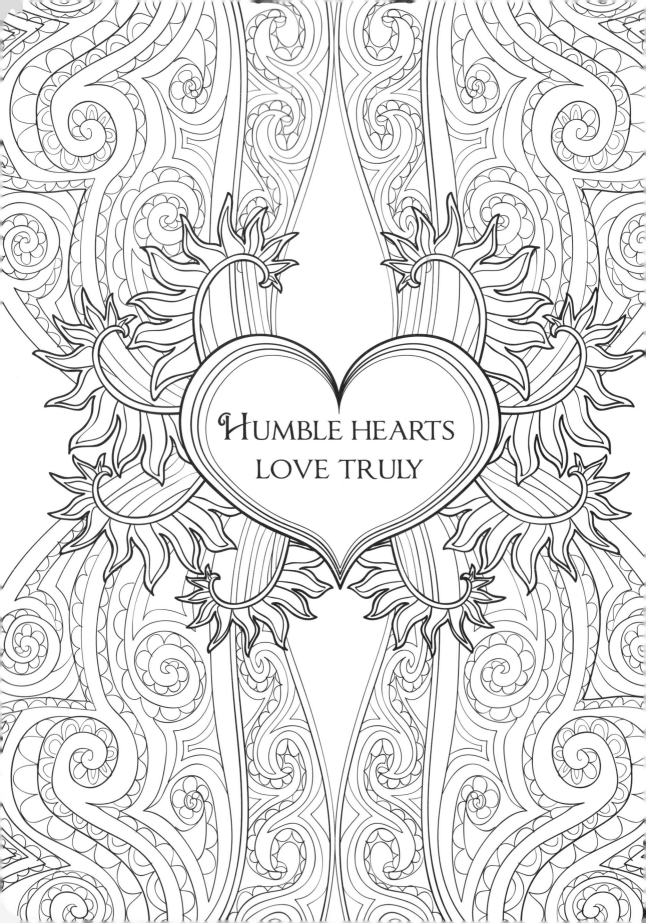

HUMBLE HEARTS
LOVE TRULY

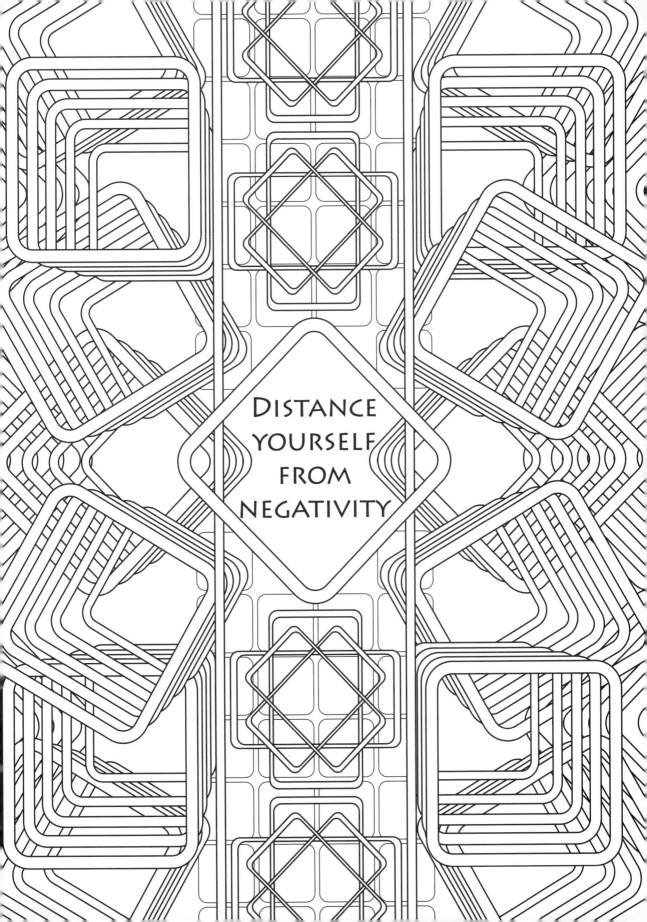

DISTANCE
YOURSELF
FROM
NEGATIVITY

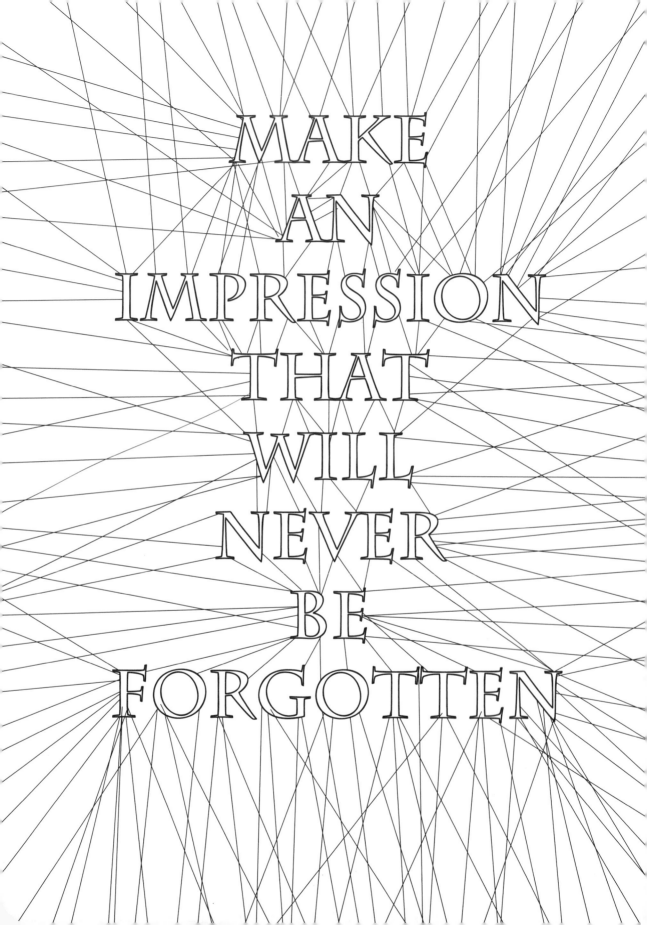

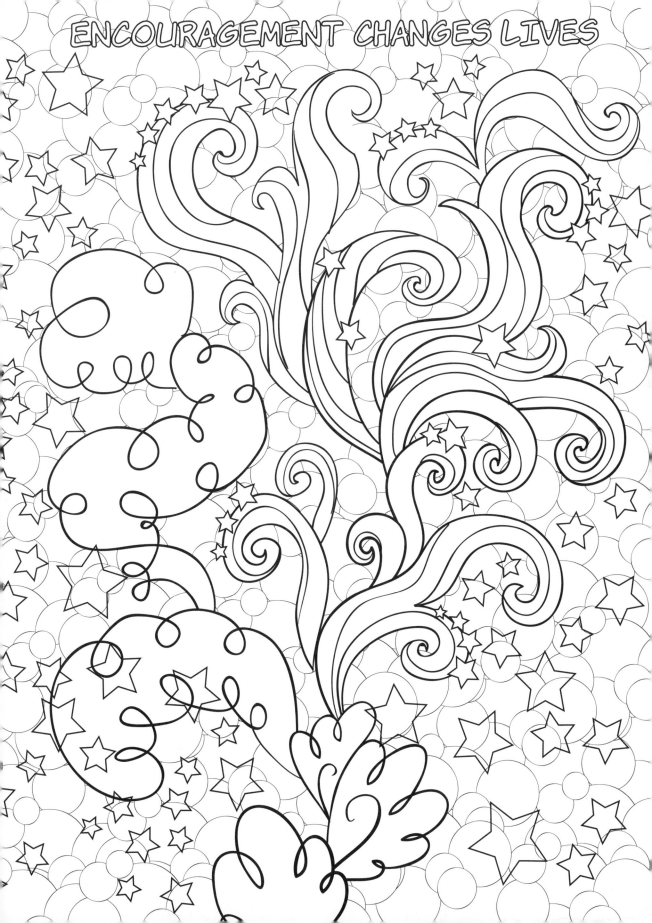

ENCOURAGEMENT CHANGES LIVES

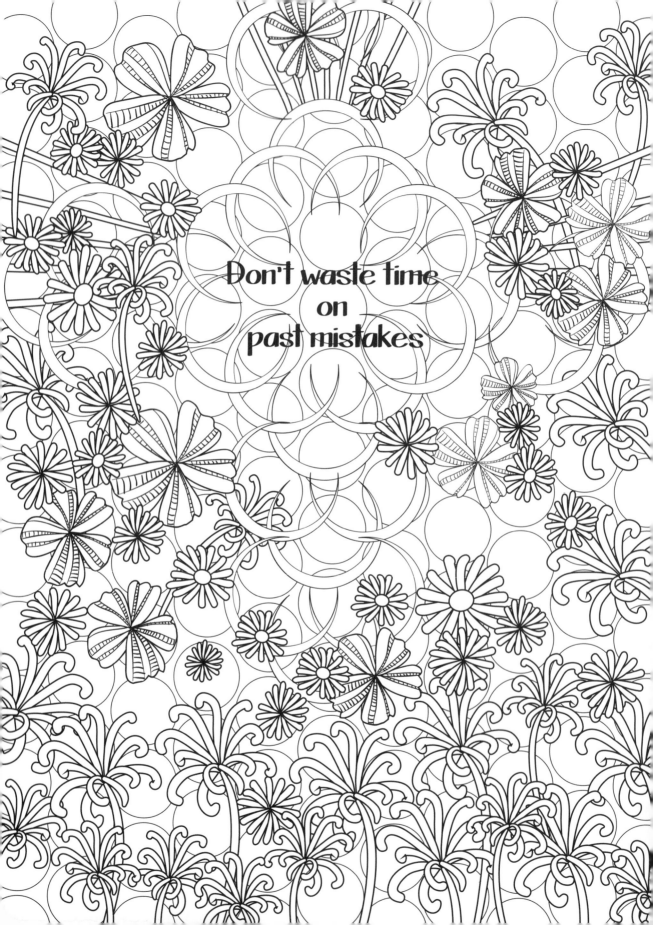

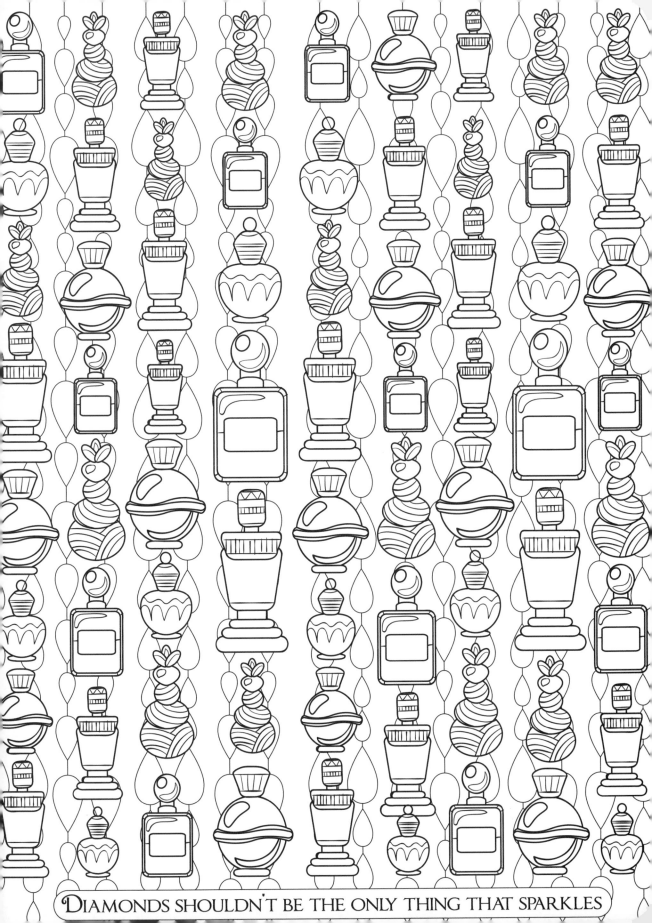

DIAMONDS SHOULDN'T BE THE ONLY THING THAT SPARKLES

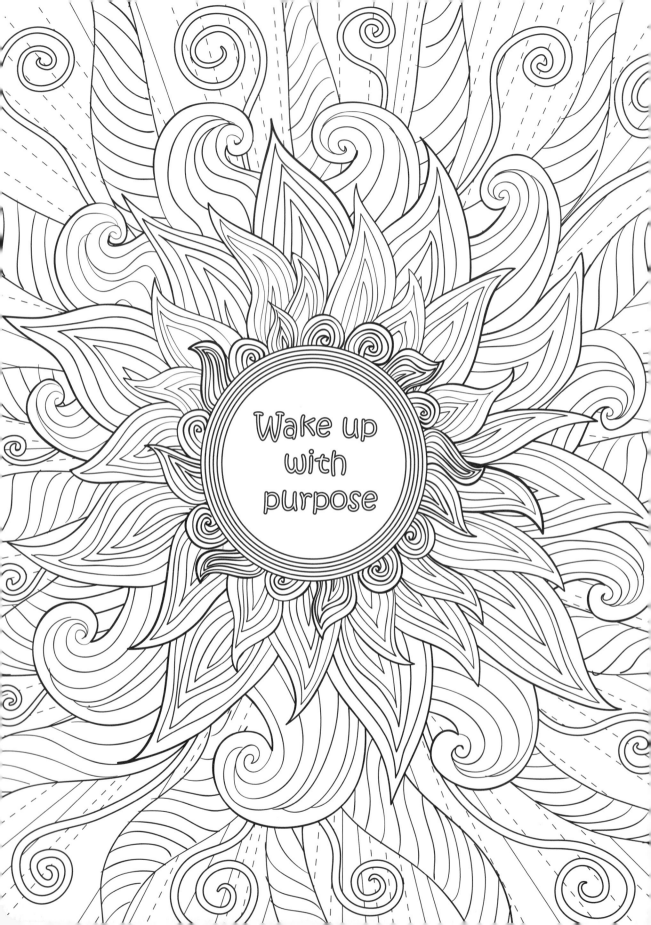

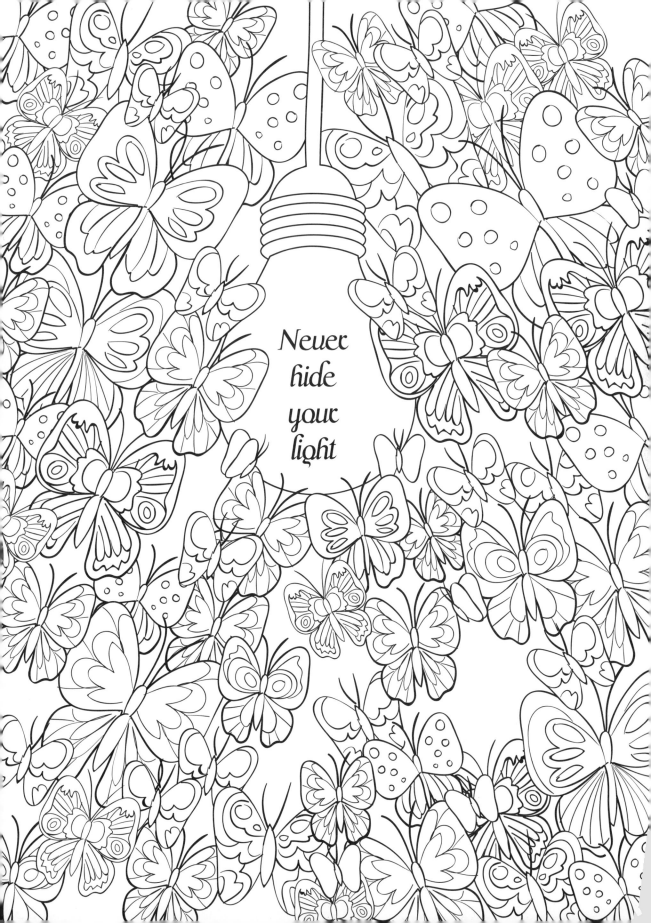

Never
hide
your
light

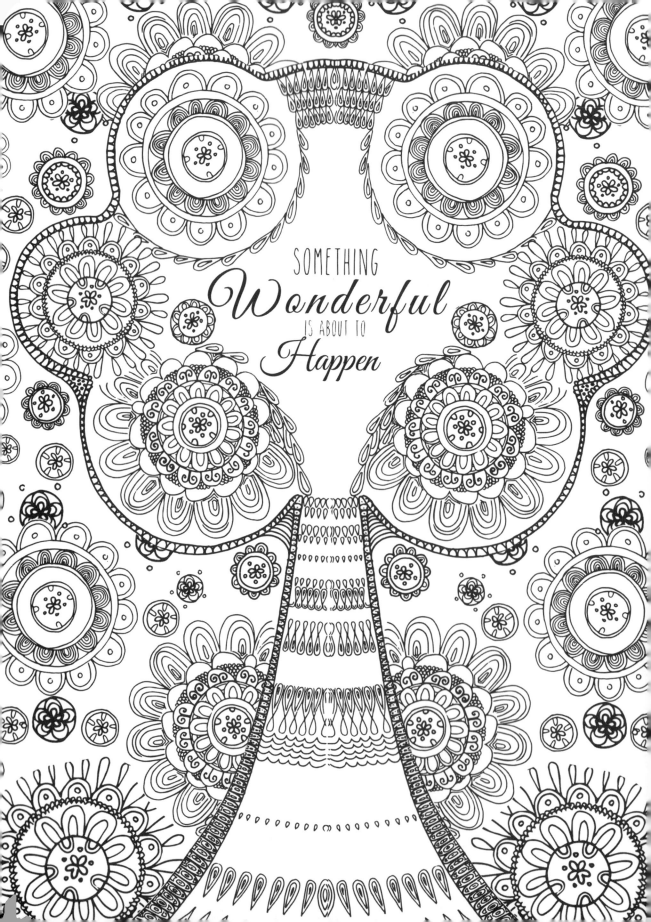

SOMETHING
*Wonderful*
IS ABOUT TO
*Happen*

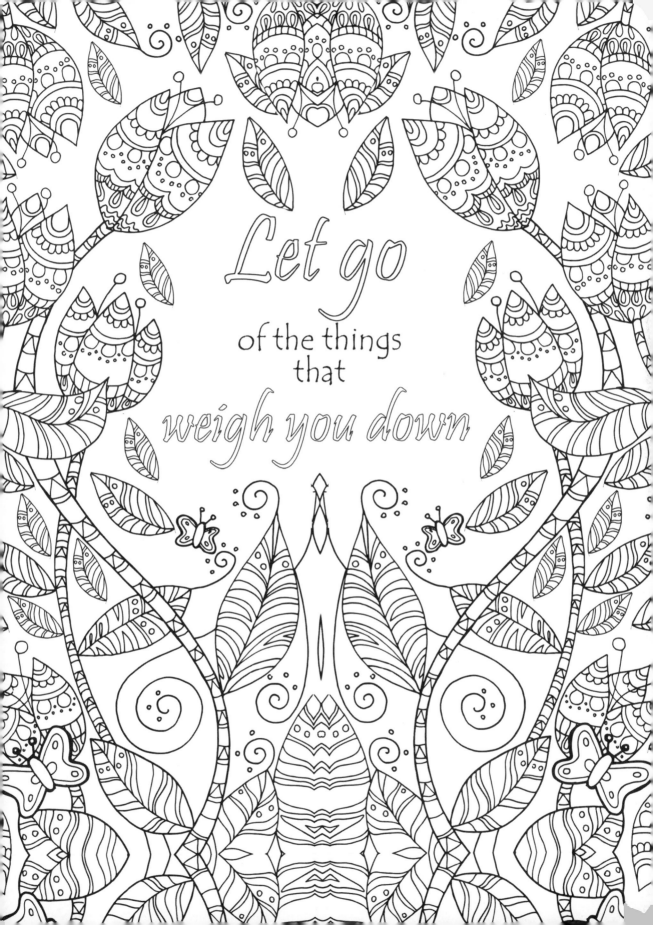

Let go
of the things
that
weigh you down

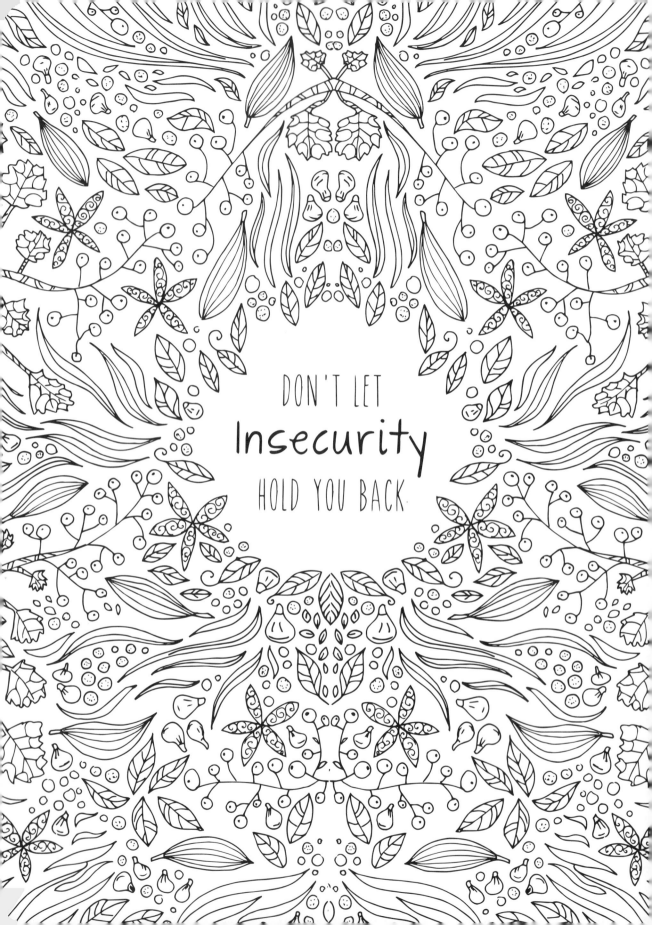

DON'T LET

Insecurity

HOLD YOU BACK

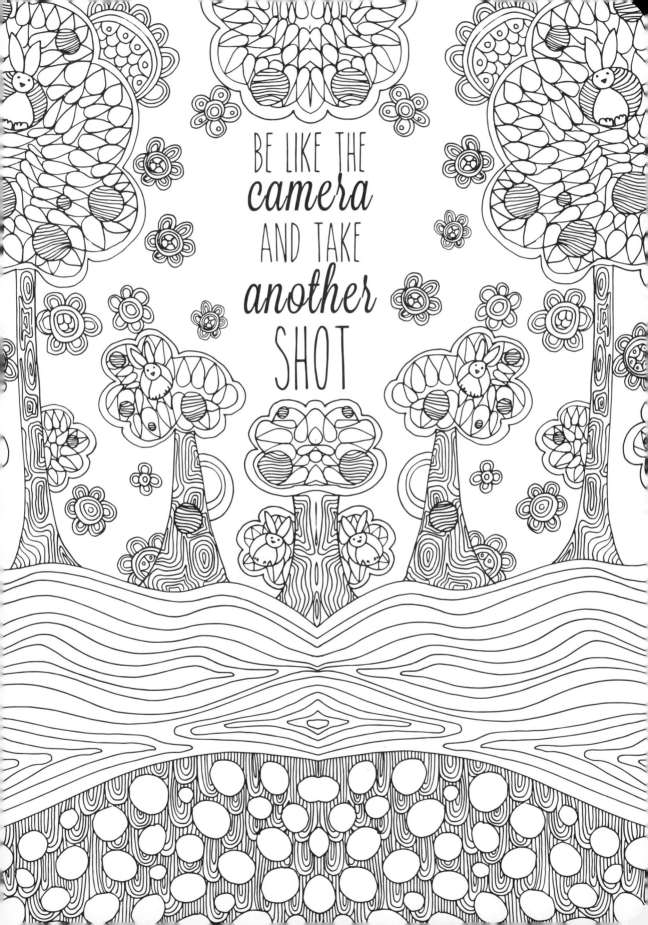

BE LIKE THE *camera* AND TAKE *another* SHOT

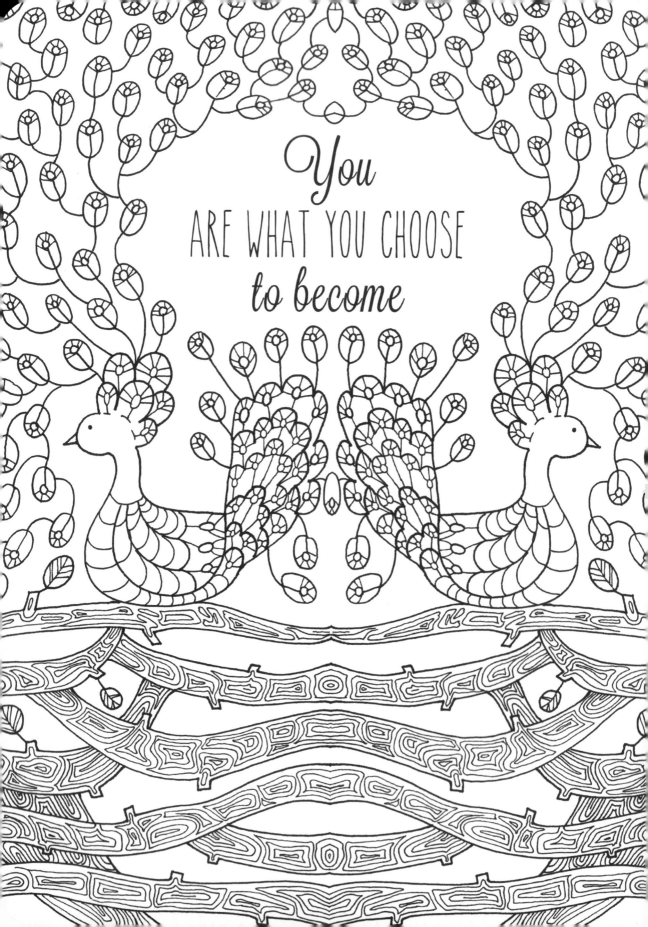

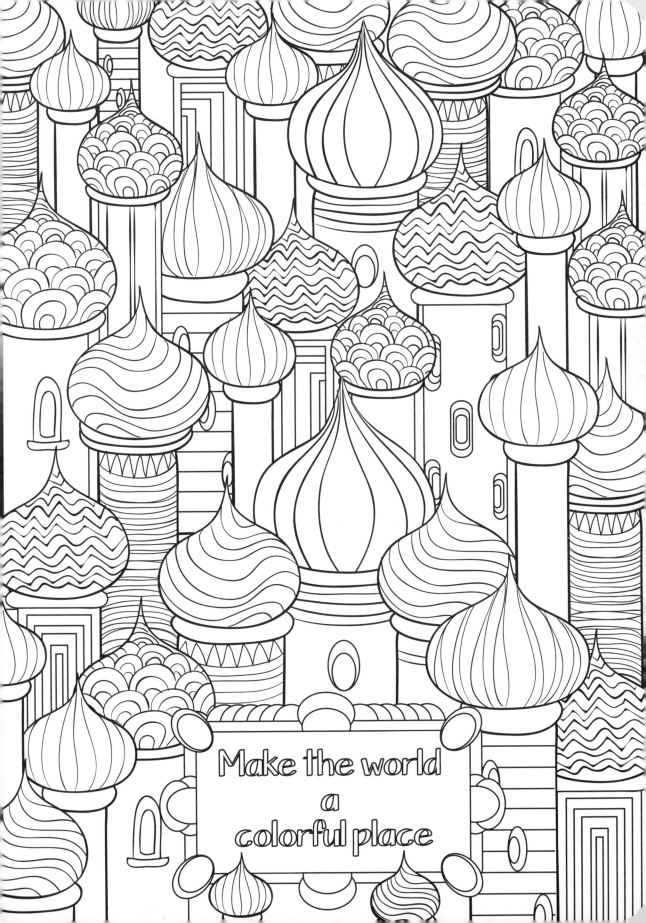

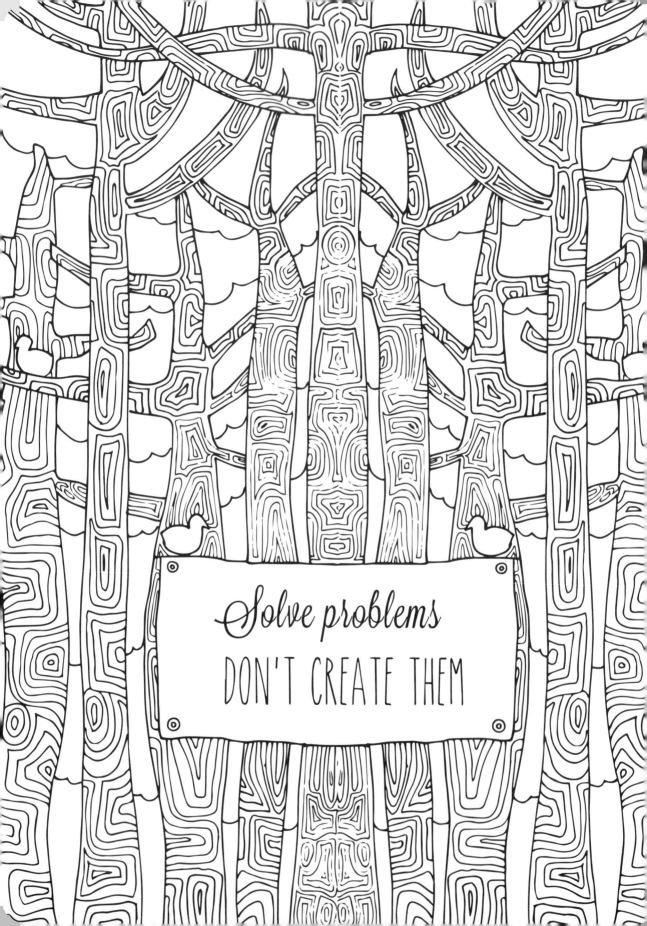

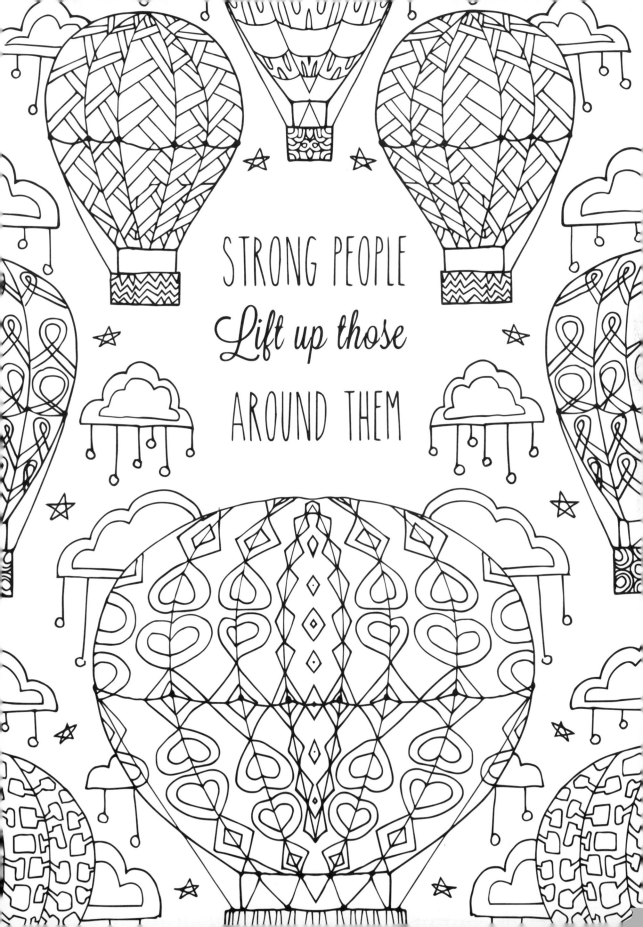

STRONG PEOPLE
*Lift up those*
AROUND THEM

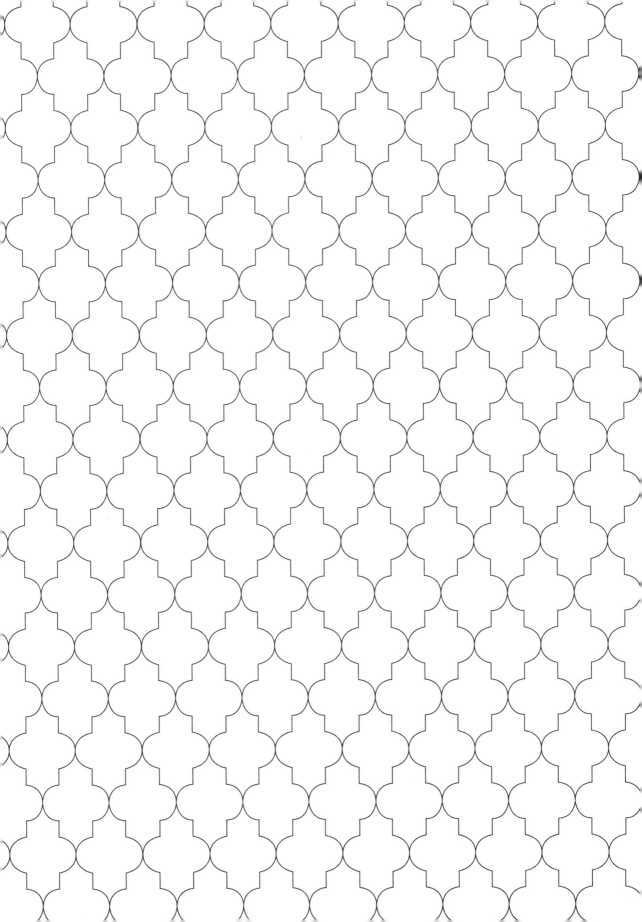

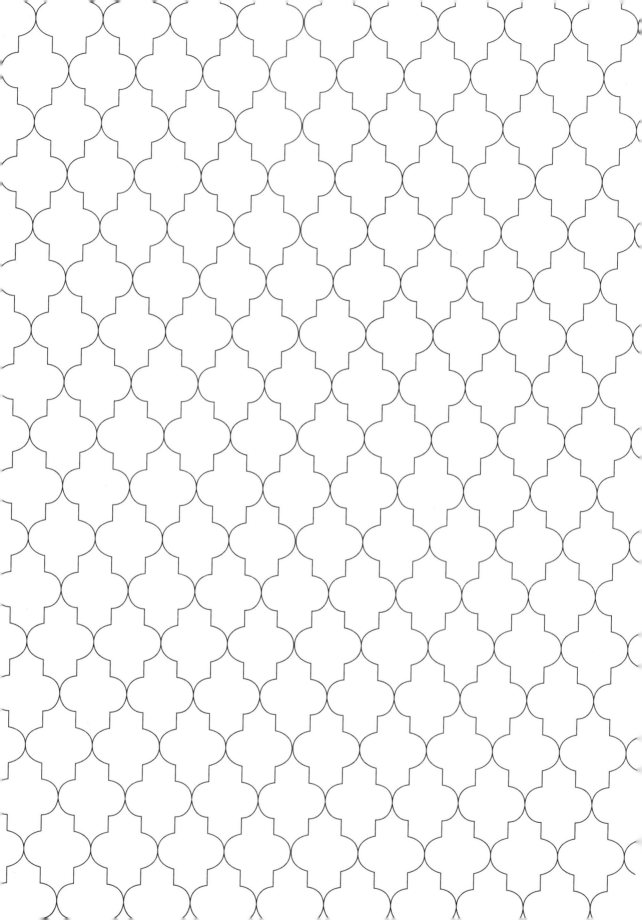